"Eric Stone's *Jumpstart Your Workplace Culture* is a great read! It offers real-world examples with practical advice feathered in to help leaders looking to transform their organization's culture. It should be 'top of the list' for anyone interested in creating a positive and productive work environment."

—**JAMES M. KERR,** TOP 10 CULTURE CHANGE THOUGHT LEADER
AND LEADERSHIP COACH

"Timeless and timely, *Jumpstart Your Workplace Culture* is a prerequisite for any leader who is trying to create a competitive advantage for their company. With a unique combination of coaching, guiding, and accountability, it's an essential blueprint for any leader trying to build a high-performance organization."

—**GARRY RIDGE,** THE CULTURE COACH & CHAIRMAN EMERITUS, WD-40 COMPANY

"In the wake of the Great Resignation, maintaining a culture where everyone is engaged continues to be a challenge for many. With this book, Eric brings a real-life approach to building—and upholding—a culture that focuses on people as well as profits and growth. People are our most valuable asset, and the book is a reminder that culture eats strategy for lunch. If you don't have a great culture in place, you won't be in business for long. Buy the book and build the best road map for your organization."

—**JEFFREY HAYZLETT,** PRIMETIME TV AND PODCAST HOST, SPEAKER,
AUTHOR, AND PART-TIME COWBOY

*To all of the businesses who are inspired
to jumpstart their workplace culture.*

www.amplifypublishing.com

Jumpstart Your Workplace Culture

Second printing. This Amplify Publishing edition published in 2023.

For more information, please contact:
Amplify Publishing, an imprint of Amplify Publishing Group
620 Herndon Parkway, Suite 220
Herndon, VA 20170
info@amplifypublishing.com

Library of Congress Control Number: 2022919370

CPSIA Code: PRV1223B

ISBN-13: 978-1-63755-396-1

Printed in the United States

JUMPSTART YOUR WORKPLACE CULTURE

A ROAD MAP
FOR IGNITING
HIGH PERFORMANCE

ERIC D. STONE

amplify
an imprint of Amplify Publishing Group

CONTENTS

INTRODUCTION

Since early 2021, we've been hearing about the Great Resignation. People, especially people under forty, have been quitting their jobs in unprecedented numbers in search of satisfaction, meaning, or more support from their companies. With that as our backdrop, have you ever wondered how some organizations keep great people, while other organizations are consistently losing them? How do they consistently perform at a high level for an extended period of time? How do they create a unique bond and sense of belonging with their employees and anyone who interacts with them? These are organizations in which employees and customers are true advocates and ambassadors—companies in which obstacles become opportunities, and the culture encourages excellence.

Is there a playbook for building that kind of culture and

organization? Can you measure culture, its impact, and its health? I think the answers to both questions are yes. I'm here to explain how and why. During my twenty-six-year tenure with Enterprise Holdings, I always considered it to be a special place. There was a sense of camaraderie that I have seen in few other organizations. It came out in the way everyone, from individual contributors to top-level managers, would pull together, have fun, support each other, and execute the plan to the highest levels of success. This example will show you what I mean.

In October 2012, Hurricane Sandy slammed into the Northeast. The region I led—which bordered the Bronx and moved north, covering most of the Connecticut coast—was devastated. Roads were impassable; people were stranded for days without power; communication was cut off; and thousands of cars were submerged beneath floodwater, including some of our fleet. Amid the chaos, my team had to serve four groups of people.

First, we had to try to get in touch with our employees to determine if they and their families were safe and who was able to come to work. Second, we had to take care of our company. We conducted inventory checks at each retail location to evaluate the condition of our fleet, identified stores that were operational, and recorded property losses. Next, we had to serve our customers, many of whose cars were either flooded or trapped under fallen tree limbs. Furthermore, with the airports shut down, thousands of other people were trapped in New York and Connecticut, and they desperately tried to rent cars to drive home.

Finally, we had to look after our business partners. We reached out to them to see how they were doing, from the status of their businesses to the condition of their homes. We also kept them informed of our inventory because their customers were going to be in dire need of transportation, and we wanted to not only understand their needs but be transparent about the accessibility of vehicles.

We operated our crippled locations without electricity or computers, relying on cell phones where we had service. Some stores were running on generators. But with most gas stations closed because the electrical grid was down, fuel was a scarce commodity. Some stores improvised, using the AC auxiliary outlets on their Dodge Caravans and Chrysler Town and Country vans to power their facilities. Employees who had grown up with computers learned how to write up manual bills on the job. Somehow we kept things running.

In my region, we repositioned employees who could commute to other stores, shipped cars all over the country to assist those hit even harder than us, and made lots of other decisions that weren't good for our bottom line but were good for our customers and employees. We changed policies on the fly, eliminating our fee for dropping off a car at a random location. We communicated with everybody constantly. We did what was necessary to serve the people we were there to serve.

We got through it. Everyone was incredibly unselfish; we all knew we would get through the ordeal together. At the branch level, had we not created a consistent level of trust, authenticity, and empathy, there was no way we would have been able to handle the long hours and challenges. To this day, I still look back in awe of how our employees rose to the challenge. The company's foundation even offered generous financial support to help neighborhoods affected by the devastating storm.

This was about more than getting someone into a replacement vehicle. Some customers were desperate to get to work or to check on a loved one. Some even said they needed the car so they would have someplace to sleep. Others would enter a location and break down in tears because they had just lost their homes and all their possessions. One gentleman came into our Stamford, Connecticut, location because he needed to check in on his grandparents, who had been stranded in Long Island for days with no power, food, or medicine. Communication was down, and this man's own car had been totaled when a giant tree fell across his driveway. The trouble was, the only car we had available was the branch manager's company car. Without hesitation, the branch manager handed over the keys to this distraught gentleman.

It's a special culture in which people can see past their individual goals in order to do the right thing for other people. That culture was our edge. The company's reputation soared after that disaster because of our culture. We didn't just survive; we thrived.

A LITTLE ABOUT ME

From a young age, I was fascinated with business. My father was a textile salesman, and every morning I would watch him put on his suit and tie and drive off to meet his clients. When he would arrive back at home after a long business trip, I would eavesdrop on his conversations with my mother about landing new accounts, dealing with difficult clients, and all the ups and downs of his work. Pretty quickly, I was hooked on everything about business.

During my senior year in college, I landed an internship at the Providence Civic Center in Rhode Island, in the group sales department. The more I learned about business, the more I was enamored with it. I loved learning about business operations—how you could improve profits with a few small tweaks, and what got people motivated to put in long hours and exceed expectations. Right after college, I was hired by Enterprise as a management trainee in the Springfield, Massachusetts, office and was fortunate to climb the corporate ladder for over two decades. Since my retirement in 2018,

I have continued to use my approach to help many nonprofit and for-profit organizations build an elite culture.

I know many people won't have the good fortune to spend their careers with one company the way I did, but that's why it's important to understand what really leads to a successful culture and makes a company—any company—run like a finely-tuned machine. Some of the ideas were all mine, others I enhanced through team collaboration. This solution, which took me decades to create, is the product of experience, trial and error, and interaction with a lot of great people.

CULTURE IS THE SECRET

After ten years at Enterprise, my superiors handed me a big task: turning around southern New England, a region that had struggled for years with employee retention, customer service, growth, and profitability. It was evident that the culture of the region was struggling and needed a change. I fine-tuned my playbook and put all the lessons I had learned into action. Gratifyingly, they worked! Not only did my team and I turn the region around but we became the region everyone strived to beat. We labeled our region 24CC—24 was our group number, and CC was shorthand for our region—and in short order we became a dynasty, the company version of the 1960s Boston Celtics.

How? Culture. Every company should be built around founding values, and those values must be the heart and soul of your culture. In everyone's personal journey, a particular value may resonate. I witnessed the ability of each individual's personal brand to shape their words and actions. I saw the importance of chemistry and teamwork, which kept people working late by choice and striving to improve out of pride. I experienced the power of consistent training and coaching.

But even though the company gave me the tools and knowledge to be a successful leader, it was up to me to use them to make my store, division, or region the best it could possibly be. In other words, they might have given me the car, but it was up to me to map out the course and drive. That's what I did with 24CC. I learned the fundamentals, but then I enhanced and expanded them. I brought ideas and initiatives to the region, and my leadership team and I applied them in ways no one at the company had ever applied them before. The result was a unique level of accomplishment that made us one of the most successful, smooth-running, and profitable regions in the history of the company.

I've written this book to teach you how we did it—how we built and sustained a culture of trust, clarity, strong communication, constant coaching, accountability, and an ownership mentality. Despite what some pundits say, corporate culture is predictable and even *measurable*. Here's how I define it:

A high-performance culture happens when a set of shared values and beliefs drives the right behaviors, creating a consistent experience and desirable outcomes.

How strong was our culture? Many employees would accept jobs claiming they would "give it a year" because they didn't see any glamour or a long-term future in "just renting cars." Then they became part of the culture, and they saw we were doing a lot more than "just renting cars." We were teaching people how to lead and achieve their true potential. Suddenly they couldn't wait to stick around and see what would happen next. They took pride in where they worked. Like me, some stayed with the company for decades.

MY CULTURE PLAYBOOK

Many people misunderstand culture. They think it's soft and philosophical, with hugs and high fives, built on rousing speeches and employees spending leisure time together. It's not. A strong culture is built on clear, high expectations, exemplary training and development, consistent follow-up, steady accountability—and trust. Culture is anything but soft. It is the catalyst for high execution. It not only eats strategy for breakfast but lunch and dinner too; however, culture is predictable and measurable. In the final chapter, you'll find my six-point inspection system, a tool for measuring the health of an organization's culture *empirically*. This unique approach assesses the health of your organization and considers six critical components that reflect what's happening inside and outside a company: employee engagement; customer satisfaction; the company's cultural values; diversity, equity, and inclusion; employee retention; and profit or growth.

In these pages, I'm going to share every detail and secret from my culture playbook with you. I think you'll be able to apply the strategies my team and I used to your own organization. While many of the tools, tactics, and lessons you'll read about are the results of experiences with one of the largest privately held companies in North America, they're universally applicable and are crucial to jumpstarting (or maintaining) the culture you strive for in your company. Whether you're in a service industry, technology, health care, media, manufacturing, or some other sector, you can make a few tweaks in my methodology and put it to work igniting your own winning culture.

These were some of the keys to my success:

- Spend time in the trenches with your people so you develop the sense you're all in this together, pulling as one.
- Design processes and systems based on solid data and experience. Coach all levels to execute the plan consistently. Hold employees accountable for the outcomes.
- Communicate relentlessly about expectations, goals, performance, everything.
- Find ways to get everyone's mind, hands, and heart engaged in the business. When people care, they show up.
- Recognize effort and reward excellence.
- Make time to have fun and connect away from work.
- Measure the health of your organization at least two times a year to ensure you're on the right path—or if you need a jumpstart.

Because every good book needs a metaphor, and because I spent more than a quarter century working for a rental car company, I decided to write this book around the theme of a road trip. I'm going to take you on your own journey. Building culture is a journey, and it doesn't really have a destination. The journey *is* the destination. There will be surprises along the way, including a few side trips. But I think you'll enjoy the ride, and in the end I'm confident you'll see culture in a new way.

I've worked in a few extras, too, kind of like road trip surprises you'd find along Route 66:

- "Off-Ramp" is a sidebar where I'll dig deeper into an important point.
- "Roadside Attraction," another sidebar, will tell a story related to the chapter material.
- "What's on the Bumper Sticker?" is a memorable, short takeaway from the chapter, inspired by the clever bumper stickers we see on cars all around us.

It all comes down to this: I want you to see that culture is not some mysterious force beyond your grasp. It's logical and predictable, and if you consistently apply proven, commonsense principles, with discipline and humanity, you can create sustained excellence. This is an on-the-ground, nuts-and-bolts owner's manual for creating culture from scratch, and I think it will be quite a ride.

Ready to hit the road?

CHAPTER 1

TAKE A TEST-DRIVE

Listen, observe, and learn so you can understand your people, your process, where you are, and where you can go.

During his twelve-year tenure as chairman and CEO of Pitney Bowes, Mike Critelli spearheaded its transformation into one of the most innovative companies in the shipping, mailing, and logistics space. He also set a lofty standard for listening to and learning about his employees, one that any leader could benefit from emulating.

For Mike, all meetings and interactions at Pitney Bowes had to have a strategic purpose. After the September 11, 2001, terrorist attacks, he started recording a weekly voice mail sent to all employees every Wednesday, a morale booster for people still shaken by the terrible events in New York and Washington, DC. When employees responded with questions, he would answer each one. But I particularly like the town hall meetings he would hold on the road, sometimes in outlier locations that didn't get a lot of love from the corporate office.

When Mike had plans to fly into the field to visit sales, service, and administrative offices to do a town hall meeting, he would arrive the evening before and meet with the region vice president for a one-on-one dinner. The next morning he would have breakfast with sales, service, and administrative management. He would then have a three-hour town hall meeting with all employees and encourage a broad question-and-answer session. Finally, he would do three to four sales or service calls, each with a different sales or service professional. He received the most robust input from this combination.

He knew some people might be intimidated by the presence of the CEO, and he knew people in some parts of the country might have trouble with English, so he would have "plants" in these town hall audiences, especially with more reticent groups, like the service and administrative employees. They would ask him tough questions, put him on the spot, get the other attendees laughing, and relax the room.

Mike also made it a habit to hold "skip level meetings," meeting regularly during a year with as many as seventy-five different Pitney Bowes employees who didn't report directly to him. This was a way to get unfiltered information from the people working on the front lines and to let them know someone was paying attention to their concerns.

GATHER INFORMATION

Mike's example illustrates the importance of the first step in igniting a winning culture: gathering information about your people so you come to understand who they are and what they need.

Think of your people as the vehicle you'll be taking on this long road trip toward success. If you were getting ready for a lengthy journey, one of the first things you would do is test-drive the vehicle that will be your means of getting from point A to point B. Is the car in good shape? Does it need repairs? Does it handle well? Does it have the features you need, or do you need an upgrade? When you take the time to listen to your people, observe them in action, and learn all about them, that knowledge will make the journey more satisfying and productive.

Mike Critelli learned that at Pitney Bowes family mattered more than anything else. "The family element was extremely important," he says. "I learned that in a lot of different ways. Coming up through the ranks, there were always second- and third-generation people working in the factory. There were brothers and sisters and cousins. When I joined the company, the CEO's oldest son was the branch manager in Syracuse. You knew family connections and family relationships mattered. It was pretty easy for me to figure out that doing things for family members would have a big impact on the company."

The power of listening to, observing, and learning about your people as a foundation of a strong culture is backed up by extensive data. According to the O. C. Tanner 2020 Global Culture Report:[1]

- A strong listening strategy within companies decreased the odds of moderate-to-severe employee burnout by 54 percent. When leaders dismissed employee opinions and ideas, however, 38 percent of employees became unmotivated.
- Only 51 percent of employees think their organization is great at listening to them, and only 56 percent feel their leaders stay in touch with what employees need.

---

1   O. C. Tanner, 2020 Global Culture Report (O.C. Tanner, 2020), https://www.octanner.com/global-culture-report.html.

- One-fifth of ideas are never heard, because employees are afraid to offer them up, and half of employees don't speak their minds at work.

Those facts and my own experiences led me to develop a process for gathering information about my people.

LISTEN, OBSERVE, AND LEARN

The listen, observe, and learn process has three parts:

1. Conduct one-on-one meetings with every person on your team. Not just your direct reports but everyone. Ideally, they would be in person, but virtual platforms are effective, too.

2. Observe your people on the job—in the field, at the peak of business, and engaged in business development activity. This not only lets you see how your team behaves under pressure but also shows whether or not they are implementing your ideas and demonstrating your organization's cultural values.

3. Meet with your top customers and vendors to take their pulse and learn how you can help them be better partners to your organization.

Let's take a closer look at the steps of the process.

STEP 1: LISTEN—ONE-ON-ONE MEETINGS

A wise man once said, "First understand, then be understood."

To that end, the culture in my region included lots of one-on-one meetings between me and many individual employees. Those meetings were about connecting and learning, but they also had a clear business purpose. I wanted to balance our employees' need to feel seen and heard with my need to learn what their capabilities were—what their potential might be. In order to be great, it was important to create psychological safety within the entire team right from the start. These one-on-ones—more than 150 of them—prompted my managerial team to implement what became known as thirty minutes of fame, which we will discuss in another chapter.

In those meetings, I would go first and let them know all about me: I'm a die-hard Boston Red Sox fan, I like rap music, and once upon a time I wore parachute pants and break-danced. The mental image of me dressed like MC Hammer never failed to draw a chuckle, and that made things easier. Then I would pivot to the employee. "I would love to learn more about you," I'd say. "I would love to find out how things are going for you, and I want you to be honest with me."

I would learn about their family situation, where they went to school, and find common ground where I could. For instance, if they told me they were the youngest in their family, I'd let them know that I am too. It was all about finding the points that would make them feel as comfortable as possible. Investing this time, and being authentic and empathetic, let each employee know that I honestly cared about their personal and professional success. I was planting seeds that might eventually grow into trust. As Harvard Business School professor Frances Frei says, "Trust has three components: authenticity, logic, and empathy. When all three of these things are working, we have great trust."[2]

As a manager, if your goal is to nurture trust, there's no substitute for talking with the people who are on the front lines of your organization and coming to understand the day-to-day challenges they face. Get to know them one-on-one, in a technically formal but low-key environment in which there's no performance review or expectations, just an honest, open conversation. You're learning, not interrogating.

Some one-on-one best practices you can use in your organization:

• Schedule your one-on-ones well in advance and use calendar software so there's no confusion. I liked scheduling a few weeks out, and I always made sure each employee knew how long the meeting would be, that this wouldn't be a performance review but a friendly chat, and that one goal would be making work better for everyone. It's never too early to start putting people at ease. Remember: a meeting with the boss is inherently stressful for most people.

• Start on time. The number-one reason meetings fail to achieve their goals is because they start late. Then the meeting is rushed or even postponed. As the leader, you're supposed to set the example. If you're late, you just tacitly told that employee that it's okay if they're late too. In the military, there is a saying: "If you are not five minutes early, you're late." Live by this ethos. Precision is a crucial component of a winning culture. Schedule precisely and be on time—no exceptions.

2   Finding Mastery, "The Power of Trust and Maximizing Potential with Frances Frei and Anne Morris," 39:50, August 11, 2021, https://findingmastery.net/anne-frances.

THINGS ABOUT YOURSELF

- Share some things about yourself. There's inherent employee angst when the boss asks for a sit-down, so it's important to defuse it. One of the best ways is to be self-deprecating about your own flaws. I've already mentioned that I talk about my parachute pants and love of rap, but there's a lot more you can talk about:
- A brief career history. Share where you've worked, where you went to school, and what you've done since you joined the company. Be as forthcoming as you want your employee to be.
- A little bit about your family and hobbies. I always wanted to ensure I was relatable to my team and that they knew we probably had a lot more in common than they thought.
- Your philosophy on business. This lets your people hear your approach toward business, performance, and accountability from you, not the grapevine.
- Your goals, expectations, and management style. Give everyone a clear picture of your approach to day-to-day operations. I would let my people know that I had very high standards, but that I would also draw them a clear road map for achieving those standards.
- "Any questions for me?" Cultivate approachability. You want your employees confiding in you, asking questions, and keeping the lines of communication open.

PERSONAL QUESTIONS

- Ask respectful personal questions. Remember: you're not interrogating this employee; however, there's nothing wrong with asking questions that tell you something about their character, values, history, and personality. This is your chance to gain a good understanding of who they are and even find common interests. This is also a good opportunity to improve your organization's diversity, equity, and inclusion by showing respect for each person's ethnicity, faith, cultural traditions, gender identification, or other unique traits. Some example questions:

- "What college did you graduate from?"
- "Where did you grow up?"
- "Tell me about your family. Brothers or sisters?"
- "What occupies your spare time? Any hobbies? Are you a fan of a sports team or a musical group? Are you obsessed with a TV show? Have a favorite book?"
- "What were you best known for in school or at your last job?" This is a great question for getting a sense of what the individual believes are their strengths—sales, customer service, employee development, etc. I always found it interesting to compare their assessment with what I had observed on my own.
- "Why did you choose to work here?" Some employees might be too honest. For example, I had one employee who said, "I was just looking for a job, and I thought I would apply." That's probably not what your boss wants to hear.

PROFESSIONAL QUESTIONS

- Ask strategic professional questions. I wanted to get their opinions and impressions of the current environment of the organization as well as get their thoughts about opportunities and challenges. It was critically important to admit I don't have all the answers and encourage the team to share their insights, questions, or concerns.
- "What's your employee experience been like so far?" This is a chance to take the temperature of your present culture and identify holes in your training, communications, or cultural road map.
- Do they know and understand the company values? If not, there is work to do on employee education.

• "Which of the company's founding values have you found to be backed up by action? In other words, where are we walking our talk?" Practically every business claims to be built on a foundation of certain values. This is a chance to find out if your company is living up to its promises, and if your employee is paying attention to the surrounding culture.

• "Which founding values are you not seeing in real life?" Hypocrisy leads to cynicism, and cynicism kills culture. It's useful to find out where the organization might be coming up short.

• "Can you articulate our current strategy?" Many times I have seen a team get frustrated with an employee only to find out the employee was never told about a strategic initiative or trained on a task. This question also helps reveal if the employee has bought into the mission or even understands the mission. Finally, you allow the employee to provide feedback on potential improvements.

• "What management style do you find most motivating?" I've coached thousands of employees, and there is no one-size-fits-all formula for bringing out someone's full potential. Despite this, I have watched managers get upset with their people over not finding the manager's motivational approach effective, when it's the manager who's at fault. Don't assume. Ask.

• "What's an opportunity the team might be overlooking right now?" You could find some nuggets that lead to profitable changes or new initiatives. You can't predict the source of a good idea.

• "Do you feel challenged and encouraged to grow?"

• "When you provide feedback, do you feel that it's taken to heart?" Culture blossoms where people feel heard, so listening without acting needs to be addressed.

• "Where do you think your team ranks?" If your company runs a sales dashboard or ranks teams by other key performance indicators (KPIs), this can be huge. You need your employees to be dialed into the company's performance. When I first arrived in my new position as regional VP, everyone assumed our region was doing very well. When I shared our poor ranking, jaws dropped. Can you imagine playing on a professional sports team and not knowing your record? Neither can I.

• "Where could you use more coaching and training?" You could find out where there are deficiencies that, if corrected, could yield performance improvements.

• "Who's been your biggest influence here?" I personally reached out to the people who were mentioned most often in answers to this question and thanked them for being such impactful mentors. You want it to be clear to your team that you're building a culture of teamwork, leadership, and a "pay it forward" mentality.

• "Is there anything you think the senior leaders don't understand?"

• Take detailed notes. At the end of your meetings, merge all the info together and identify trends. This also enables you to keep important personal information about each employee at your fingertips. Taking notes also shows you're listening actively and taking the time seriously. Some of the most positive changes I made within my region came from one-on-ones.

The true goal of these one-on-ones is to lay the groundwork for trust, to understand each employee and their needs, to help them understand the opportunities and challenges, and to gauge their awareness of the organization's strategies and their ability to play their part in moving toward individual and team goals. You're also trying to determine the long-term potential of each person on your team. Is this someone who could stay at your company for ten years?

OFF-RAMP

Use the personal information you get about each employee to create a profile of each person with important facts—birthdays, anniversaries, what college they went to, and so on. Use whatever tool is easiest for you, from a yellow pad and file folders to the internet. Great leaders make the effort to make personal connections at just the right time.

For example, suppose you find out your employee went to a university whose basketball team just won a big game in the NCAA tournament. Saying, "Paul, congratulations on the big win by Syracuse!" at a team event shows genuine interest and care. Even taking the time to get to know the name of your employee's significant other scores big. People appreciate being seen as more than just cogs in a machine. If you collect all this personal information and don't use it, you're wasting a tremendous opportunity to strengthen your culture.

By the way, it might seem like a small thing, but include the proper spelling and pronunciation of each person's first and last name. Few things are more embarrassing than handing someone a plaque or sending a nice email and spelling their name incorrectly. I was obsessive about this.

How about your own ERM system (employee relationship manager), similar to what Salesforce uses with CRM (customer relationship management)?

STEP 2: OBSERVE—WATCH YOUR PEOPLE IN ACTION

To acquire knowledge, one must study;
but to acquire wisdom, one must observe.
—Marilyn vos Savant

Observation is the other tool in your information-gathering kit. You need to know how your people are behaving in real time: what choices they are making, how they are dealing with customers, and how well they are solving problems and leading others. The most effective way to do that is to get into the field regularly and watch them work. That will give you a clearer sense of how your people are implementing your plans and procedures and adhering to your organization's core values on the job. You can't lead a customer-facing workforce if all you do is sit in your office.

The most useful information I received about how I could help my region improve was always this observational data. In getting into the field and watching my team in action, my goal was to either confirm what I believed about my people or get a dose of reality. For example, I needed to know how employees were interacting with customers. Did a location need more people? Was there a problem that required more training?

I divided my observation process into two parts: field operations and external relationships.

FIELD OPERATIONS

When I became regional VP of the southern New England region, observation was a running theme every time I was in the field, and preparation was critical. In order to be prepared for my visits to the branches in my region, I reviewed all the training our employees had gone through at each level of their careers. I can't stress enough the importance of this step. It gave me a high-level view of what employees were being taught and the initiatives they were expected to execute while running their business.

Everything was about alignment. Behaviors in the field were

supposed to align with the training employees were receiving, and my primary goal was to discover in what ways training and execution could be better aligned. To further that goal, before I made my field visits, I created a one-page document that laid out the goals, strategies, and tactics to which the team had committed. That way, I could check alignment at a glance.

A typical trip into the field would entail a visit to a retail branch to do the following:

- Open the day by observing behaviors during times of peak branch traffic.
- Use the slower midday to conduct one-on-one meetings.
- Visit the branch's top clients and vendors.
- Attend high-impact meetings with area managers——our equivalent of a district manager—and other key personnel to talk about trends, problems, and solutions.
- End the day observing closing procedures.

Observing your people can be hard because you have to watch interactions go wrong, and people make mistakes. Could I have intervened when a transaction was going south at a branch? Sure, but that's not how people learn. When you see an employee make a mistake, wait until the end of the encounter to see if the team and its leaders use the event as a coachable moment. Mistakes will happen. But if someone provides the appropriate guidance to avoid them from happening repeatedly, they can be tremendous learning opportunities.

By getting into the field, your main objective is to observe *behaviors*. Who are the talented individuals in the organization who could use a new challenge? How adept are your managers or other leaders at coaching, motivating, and communicating with their direct reports? Is the team at a certain location not following customer service procedures, and if not, why not? Some additional questions to ask when you're observing:

- Have clear expectations been set? I have seen situations in which a manager either had no idea of the goals and expectations for the location, or they didn't care about them. Either shows a lack of engagement, training, accountability, or urgency. I had other employees who shouted out the regional goals with pride, only to find out they weren't even close.
- Is everyone communicating? The day's challenges, issues, goals, roles, and responsibilities should be known by everyone on the team.
- Is there a plan for dealing with surges in business, equipment failures, being short-staffed, or other common challenges? I've seen businesses that were almost military in their discipline and preparation, and others where employees were always running late, managers complained about being short on staff or resources, and there always seemed to be a crisis brewing.
- Is there a culture of empowerment in which people are encouraged to solve problems? I saw plenty of teams in which everyone depended on the leader to fix things—a sign of a dysfunctional culture.
- Is there an ownership mentality? Do employees try to go above and beyond for their customers or fellow employees as though this were their business?
- Is there coaching happening in real time? You want your supervisors or managers to be ready to coach an employee on the spot to correct a mistake. That's how learning sticks. I'm looking for an environment in which employees are encouraged to stretch their talents even if they mess up. When they do, they should receive coaching that guides them, not embarrasses them.

Your team will be on its best behavior when you're on-site. If procedures aren't being followed, or the plan isn't being properly executed with you right there observing, you can be sure things are not being done the right way when you're not there. If you see repeated failures to meet expectations, and no one says anything about it or takes the initiative to correct the failures, you can safely assume you have a problem with communication, training, or leadership. You likely also have a cultural deficit too.

For me, the real revelations came when stores were dealing with heavy customer traffic. People's true habits show up under pressure. Imagine that it's Monday morning, business travelers have arrived in Hartford by the planeload, we've opened and closed one hundred transactions already, and the phone is ringing off the hook. Are employees still following procedures and customer service protocols, or have they been exposed to poor planning? Does this location need streamlined processes or new IT tools? You can't get that business intelligence at thirty thousand feet; you have to be on the ground.

Field visits were also opportunities for me to hand out pats on the back for good work. Sometimes I wouldn't see some branch employees for two or three months, and it was vital for them to know that when they did something right I would take notice. That's *symmetry*, balancing corrective action with praise and recognition.

Some of the biggest, most successful brands in the world are great about handing out praise. One day an excited Hewlett-Packard engineer ran into the office of a senior executive to announce he'd found a solution to a major problem. The manager, in the middle of eating his lunch, grabbed a banana and handed it to the employee, saying, "Well done!" Now HP gives out the **Golden Banana Award** for informal recognition of excellence. Disney hands out the coveted **Spirit of Fred Award,** named after an employee who'd been promoted and wanted to create an award recognizing the qualities he used to rise through the ranks: friendly, resourceful, enthusiastic, and dependable.

Strategic praise is another great tool for getting the most out of field operations visits. I'm not just coming to your location to point out all the things you're doing wrong. If I see something done right, I'll let you and everyone else know about it. This also reminds people, "Yes, I will notice and speak up when you're knocking the ball out of the park, but I'm going to notice when something needs improvement, or you need additional training."

EXTERNAL RELATIONSHIPS

A few years in as VP, our sales culture needed a spark. There was a lot of pressure on sales reps to report on their activity in the marketplace, but it became obvious that rather than enter detailed updates of their sales calls many reps were just entering insignificant data into our sales management system. I, along with our area and regional managers, read the status updates from our reps and watched them call on clients—*customers* were the people who walked into our branches to rent cars; *clients* were the businesses that referred customers to us—and it quickly became clear their data was just "small talk" that had nothing to do with communicating our major initiatives and the goal of becoming a true indispensable business partner. Their preparation was hit or miss—it was a case of "garbage in, garbage out."

Once we knew the situation, senior leadership and I took a time-out. We realized that not only was this an opportunity to coach our salespeople and correct shortcomings in their preparation and execution but we could use this knowledge to develop new sales trainings and build momentum through repetition and incentives. We sat down and came up with new tools for our salespeople: keys to preparation, talking points addressing our value proposition, and more. Our goal wasn't to tell them how to sell but to coach them on the right behaviors that would lead to a positive outcome.

To make sure our reps approached this challenge with enthusiasm, we also created a monthly effective sales call tracker for each branch. This spreadsheet not only showed the number of total sales calls from the previous month but also broke those calls down based on the percentage of *effective* and *ineffective* sales calls to our clients. An effective sales call was one that gained more business, provided value, and continued to build on prior updates. Now, at a glance, we could see which branches were meeting or falling short of expectations—and so could our salespeople. These became very effective KPIs for our business. An area manager would read through the sales calls for each week to make sure each sales rep was following our new strategies and coaching advice, and the rep who had the best individual outcome would be awarded the "Marketing Story of the Week."

Once this new approach was in place, it was "lather, rinse, repeat." We *always* observed our sales reps in the field. We *always* reviewed the strategies and outcomes of their sales calls. We *always* reinforced our training at every opportunity. In this way, we got everyone pulling their oar in the same direction, which created momentum for our new sales culture and helped us transform the region.

Reinventing our sales culture also meant that senior leaders began accompanying one or more members of a branch's sales team on sales calls to important clients. The objective was to see how well each sales rep was adhering to our new sales trainings and procedures. I highly recommend doing this in addition to observing frontline employees dealing with your customers. You might join your sales team on an important marketing call with one of your top accounts, and as you observe how the call progresses you will get the answers to some important questions:

- How well did the rep prepare for the sales call?
- Did they follow your organization's carefully crafted sales process, or did they abandon that process and improvise?
- Were they prompt, concise, and pleasant?
- Did they have the information they needed at their fingertips?
- How did they handle objections?
- Did they close the sale?
- What's their follow-up plan?

ROADSIDE ATTRACTION

The thirty-second story. This was one of our key coaching and feedback tools. Suppose an employee has an upcoming transaction—in this case, let's say it's a loan officer handling the closing for a home mortgage. Beforehand, a manager or other leader would coach that employee a little bit about what to expect and how to handle the transaction. What do they know about the customer? What sales prompts or follow-up questions should they ask? What would they do to provide exemplary service? This quick, proactive coaching helps address problems before they happen, reinforcing positive behavior that leads to positive outcomes.

STEP 3: LEARN—SOLICIT FEEDBACK FROM TOP CLIENTS AND VENDORS

Finally, when you're going all in on building a strong, rich culture, you must get honest input from your best customers or clients. This gives you a point of view on the organization and its performance from outside the company, where groupthink or peer pressure can influence people's responses. In other words, if you want to know what you could do better, your clients will be happy to tell you.

We always asked for feedback from our referring clients and vendor partners. There is no better way to get useful feedback than to get it in person, but sometimes that's not possible, so take customer and vendor input however you can get it: face-to-face, over the phone, or in some cases even over a remote meeting platform, like Zoom. It's not only vital to know if you're living up to your commitments to your clients and the community but it's also important to get out of the echo chamber.

You might also combine these client and vendor visits by having a sales rep join you on some of your appointments. This gives you the opportunity to witness the dynamics of the relationship between your salesperson and the client or vendor contact. Of course, taking these meetings with a nervous sales rep can lead to some interesting findings: I once went to visit a VIP account with an employee, and instead of introducing me, who the account had never met, he introduced himself!

Holding such meetings alone has its upsides: you will tend to get more candid feedback because the account isn't feeling uncomfortable about being fully transparent. Whether you're solo or with an employee, in person, over the phone, or on Zoom, there are some questions you should always ask. When possible, ask customers to provide a concrete example that's triggered their response:

- "What challenges are you facing in your industry?" If they explain their needs, you stand a better chance of satisfying those needs.
- "What could we do to provide greater value and complement your business?" In other words, where are you messing up, and what could you do better?
- "If you could change anything about our company, what would it be?" If you're trying to build a strong culture, you must continue to raise the bar.
- "When a problem arises, have you usually been satisfied with the response time and solution? Who do you call to solve it?" You want to let the customer know you're fully invested in making life better for them. I also wanted to know if my customers had a good relationship with their local contact.

Another of my favorite tools for learning more about our clients and vendors was the relationship survey. My team would break down our clients and vendors into categories. This would allow us to customize our questions in order to be mindful of the different needs certain sectors may have. The client or vendor would answer on a scale ranging from strongly disagree to strongly agree, and the results would give us a snapshot of how our customers and vendors viewed our relationship. I recommend doing this sort of survey at least once a year to keep your finger on the pulse of your client relationships.

This is the general framework of questions we used to make sure we stayed on the right track with our clients and vendors:

- My business has an open, working relationship with the local office of Company X.

- Management has a sense of urgency when it comes to my issues and concerns.
- I feel the local office and its people appreciate my business.
- Company X consistently provides timely, high-quality service.
- I see value in Company X as a business partner.
- I advocate and refer Company X to my customers.

When soliciting client or vendor opinions, and if you're fortunate enough to meet in person, remember you can often get better results if you get out of the business environment. Go to lunch or grab a coffee. It's a better venue for people to open up and tell you what they really think. You also eliminate potential distractions from employees and customers who might be stopping by the office. If you have time, organize an off-site meeting with a mix of customers, clients, vendors, and a few members of your leadership team. This group can act as your advisory board or focus group. I have done this in the nonprofit world, where we will meet with a few key stakeholders, board members, community partners, and staff to get valuable feedback on the organization. Is there clarity and alignment with our mission and vision? Are we living up to our commitments? What are our strengths, weaknesses, opportunities, and threats?

▲ ROADSIDE ATTRACTION

By listening, observing, and learning during one of our sales calls with a major client, we found out they were in desperate need of an employee. Instead of just being empathetic, we surprised them the following day—thanks to the unselfish behavior of our TA (talent acquisition) department, who worked their magic. We handed out five qualified résumés for their open position and helped them to hire a top-notch employee. Talk about a memorable moment that built loyalty and cemented our relationship!

SYMBIOSIS

One of the keys to successfully using the listen, observe, and learn method to gather actionable information about your organization is to make all your tactics work *symbiotically*—to design them so they work together, cross-train, and reinforce each other. In my region, one-on-ones, field observations, and learning from our marketplace partners were always symbiotic.

During every field visit, we followed a similar routine: observing a branch at peak traffic, followed by one-on-one meetings and sales calls, and then observing the branch's closing procedures. Everything my management team and I learned from these information-gathering efforts went into activities that enhanced and complemented one another. We turned data and insights into training programs for all levels and covered what we learned in our "big rock meetings"—the five meetings that drove the region's behaviors. We coached, guided, and gave feedback. Because of this constant process of cross-pollination, awareness and understanding of the key drivers of our business were embraced and executed at a high level.

The methods of listen, observe, and learn are especially useful if you're new to a department or to the organization. They'll give you a crash course in your people's character and capabilities, your field operations, your customer relationships, and a lot more. But you could be with a company for ten years and still benefit from the insights you'll gain by meeting with people, observing them in the field, and talking with your customers and vendors. The deep understanding you will gain will help you develop more precise, effective strategies for reaching your destination.

IN THE REARVIEW MIRROR

- The listen, observe, learn process is the key to gaining a deeper understanding of every facet of your organization.
- Listening revolves around extensive one-on-one interviews and mindful questions designed to reveal important professional and personal information about the employee. Encourage the team to share their insights, questions, or concerns.
- Observing falls into two large categories: field operations, which involve going to frontline locations to watch employees work, and external relationships, which involve overseeing sales calls.
- Learning comes from sitting down with major clients and vendors and finding out what you're doing right—and more importantly, what you're doing wrong.
- The business intelligence you gather from listen, observe, learn should be used symbiotically, each finding showing up in training, communications, procedures, meetings, and more, each initiative reinforcing the next.

CHAPTER 2

HOLD A SUMMIT TO FINALIZE YOUR ROAD MAP

*Determine where you're going and create a clear,
precise plan to help you and your team get to the
destination while hitting important milestones
along the way.*

n 2019 Tim Baxter retired as president and CEO of Samsung Electronics North America. He enjoyed a long tenure of achievements at the helm of one of the leading consumer products brands in the world. But when I sat down to interview Tim about culture and what makes it tick, the conversation quickly turned to the Galaxy Note 7 recall crisis.

In August 2016, Samsung released its Galaxy Note 7 phone to wide acclaim and record-breaking sales in South Korea. Unfortunately, reports started coming in that the phone's battery sometimes overheated, occasionally leading to fires and explosions. By

September, the company had voluntarily recalled about 2.5 million phones, but at the same time US aviation authorities and some airlines started telling passengers not to turn on their phones or use them on planes—a PR nightmare. On September 15, the Consumer Product Safety Commission issued a formal recall of the Galaxy Note 7.

This was a major crisis for Samsung, and it was Tim's job to manage it and contain the damage. During my time in corporate America, I found the key to getting through tough times was picking the right path and creating a road map. Put policies and procedures in place, keep things simple, execute relentlessly over and over again, and ingrain the right habits in everyone. That way, when the unexpected happened, and the pressure was on, we knew what to do.

When I shared my road map approach with Tim, he recognized it immediately. "The value of that couldn't have been more evident than when I was leading the company through the Note 7 recall and crisis," he said in our interview. "It was literally one hundred days in a war room, sometimes all night. During that hundred-plus days, I only had one meeting that didn't relate to the crisis."

Tim told me the greatest lesson of that time was learning how to operate in a nonlinear environment, according to a plan. He was leading a team of sixty stressed-out people in a room, with meals being brought in all day and nobody getting much rest. He was ordering PR teams to have communication plans drafted in ninety minutes while getting real-time updates on battery tests. "These things would take days or weeks in a normal environment," he said. "Here we were acting like a start-up. We got more things done than I could've ever imagined during the crisis. We spent a lot of time afterward saying, 'How do we bottle some of that?'"

Tim concludes, "Even though you can't operate in war zone crisis mode all the time, you can cut through a lot of the BS and become more efficient, more effective, and focus on what matters."

GATHER AND COMMIT

No matter how you measure your progress from point A to point B, you can't simply dictate a plan to your team. If you want your people to adopt a plan without resistance and with enthusiasm, they need to feel like their voice was heard and that they were involved in its development. So, when you have turned raw data and your insights into a comprehensive strategy for your region, department, or company, it's time to call a meeting to begin developing the road map for your journey.

A road map summit is a time to gather and commit. It's an opportunity to answer questions, create clarity, begin training on the details of the plan, and begin the repetition that leads to proficiency. It's also a chance to let people know they played a key role in shaping the plan they'll be expected to follow. By gathering everyone together to commit to your plan, you'll set clear expectations for the coming days, weeks, and months and ensure that everyone is on board with your vision.

Some people dislike meetings, but I found properly conducted meetings with precise agendas and goals to be invaluable tools for sustaining culture, setting objectives, and creating the road map for my region. Organized, communicative meetings let me ensure that everyone understood their role in achieving our success and was fully invested in that success. For this to happen, everyone had to grasp how individual goals supported branch goals, how branch goals supported area goals, and how area goals fed the goals of our region.

A road map summit is not a time for taking more feedback or revising the plan, however. During the listen, observe, learn stage of my process, I had already held more than 150 face-to-face meetings with everyone on my team—including all my regional, area, and branch managers—and made numerous observational visits to branch locations. I had spent a great deal of time learning about the challenges the people on my team faced and soliciting their thoughts and feedback on how we could improve operations. The entire process took about two months.

By the time I got to the summit meeting, I had synthesized the data and put together our strategic plan. The goal was to walk everyone on my team through the road map we would implement together. This was a crucial building block and my first opportunity to get my entire management team together to finalize our road map. Everyone played a role in designing the final document, but I put my unique personal signature on every page.

WHAT'S ON THE BUMPER STICKER?

MEETING TIP

Have a brief time gap between your listen, observe, learn phase and your road map summit meeting. This demonstrates you're keeping the process moving and drives a sense of urgency.

GUIDING PRINCIPLES

A road map says more than, "This is where we're going, this is how we'll get there, and this is where we'll stop to take a break." A plan with a clear strategy, methods, and expectations is the founding document of your culture. It's your constitution. It determines not only how you and your team will get things done on days when things go as expected but on those days when things appear to be falling apart. With the right road map in place, executed with discipline and consistency, you could end up with something like Tim Baxter's extraordinary Samsung crisis team.

A successful road map summit should run like a well-designed corporate training seminar. It should be efficient, productive, informational, and guided by a strict set of underlying business principles:

1. The key values that drive your organization's culture.

2. Your philosophy on each core area of the business.

3. Goals, both long and short term.

4. The broad vision for the organization or for your team. What does success look like, and how will you know when you get there?

5. General playbooks for everyone on the team, including its leaders. We called these our commitments.

1. BEGIN WITH VALUES

Your road map must be concise, comprehensive, and clear, but it should also reflect your organization's central values—the touchstones of how you do things and why. As we'll discuss in more detail in chapter 5, your values guide how your people should do things, help them know what to care about, and even suggest what lines they should not cross.

Values should drive everything the organization does. One great example of this is online footwear king Zappos, famous for having a creative, democratic culture. One of its core values is "Deliver

WOW Through Service." That means do something above and beyond what's expected to blow the customer's mind. To make that happen, even low-level Zappos employees are empowered to do things like giving refunds on the spot, with no "talking to my manager" excuses.

If you're working in a culture that's dysfunctional and needs transformation, start with a close look at the values that govern your organization. Are they clear? Are they authentic? Do your people even know what they are? That's not me being flippant. According to a survey from Eagle Hill Consulting, barely half of US employees—just 53 percent—know their employer's core values.[3] That's dangerous. Ensure that your values reflect what people care about, that they're clearly and consistently communicated, and that your people understand how those values translate into behavior.

2. YOUR BUSINESS PHILOSOPHY

How do you approach each core area of the business and team you're managing? What are your guiding principles regarding customer service, sales, personnel, technology, R and D, or any other areas of business that are relevant to your team's day-to-day experience? Be sure you're clear on your governing philosophy for each one, and then communicate that philosophy unambiguously to your team.

At this point I also introduced the five factors of engagement to my team, which I will talk more about in a later chapter:

- A strong relationship with your manager. Communication, understanding, trust, and mutual respect work wonders.

---

3   Eagle Hill Consulting, "Nearly half of US workforce unsure of employers' core values," *Eagle Hill Consulting,* accessed January 25, 2023, https://www.eagle-hillconsulting.com/news/half-us-workforce-unsure-employers-core-values/.

- Clear communication of expectations and goals. There should be no confusion among your people about their role or what's expected of them.
- The right materials, equipment, and information to achieve desired outcomes. Teams should have the resources, data, technology, and training to get the job done at a high level.
- A manager who encourages personal and professional growth. Your goal is to coach and mentor individual contributors to reach their potential and advance in the organization.
- A system in which top performance is recognized. You consistently call out and reward excellence, incentivizing people to give their very best.

The factors that keep your team or workforce engaged might not be the same as these five, but it's worth investing the time to discover what the factors of engagement are for your organization.

3. GOALS

Your long-term goals are the destination for this road trip—for instance, the market share you want to own in two years. To reach those goals, you'll also need to establish a series of short-term goals for sales, service, hiring, cost savings, whatever metrics make sense for your organization or team. Your goals will determine the strategies and tactics that make up your plan. Some other metrics you might find it useful to keep an eye on as you're setting short-term goals:

- net profit and gross margin
- customer retention
- employee retention
- year-over-year revenue

- year-over-year—or quarter-to-quarter—sales growth
- Net Promoter Score
- customer acquisition cost
- employee engagement scores

4. YOUR VISION

What does the big picture look like for your team, department, or business? Do you want to be the juggernaut division within your company, the one that wins all the performance awards and sets the pace for everyone else? Do you aspire to build your small business into a beacon of technological innovation? Do you see your department breaking new ground in efficiency, cost savings, and productivity, driving higher profits and a doubling of your company's share price?

As the leader, your vision is the only one that matters to your team. It's their guiding star. Make sure it's clear to you and compelling to them, and communicate it relentlessly.

5. COMMITMENTS

This is your road map. Commitments are the tactics you and your team agree to adopt in each core area of your business in order to achieve expected results. For example, in our road map summit, we would commit to the following:

- Employee retention: Thirty minutes of fame meetings twice per month, meet your mentor meetings monthly, all employees to be up-to-date on timelines.
- Customer service: Weekly review of our five key touch points to execute our cycle of service, recognize MVPs of the week to incentivize employees to live up to our high standards, review the use of technology such as wireless devices to improve the customer experience.

- Revenue and expense: Monthly financial reviews—deep dives into our costs and sales numbers to find successes and opportunities. Daily huddles would happen every morning for the week, and the topics would alternate—Monday and Wednesday on sales, Tuesday and Thursday on cost control, and Fridays on customer service. The goal was to keep the content topical and coachable so it would resonate with everybody in attendance.

- Market growth: Monthly meetings that looked at what we were doing in the marketplace, reviewed our goals, and examined KPIs, like number of effective sales calls per month, hours spent on sales per month, whether or not our sales reps hit all the action steps in our sales strategy.

REST STOP

When you're on a long road trip, you've got to make periodic stops to check the map or GPS—if you're in a place where you have cell service—and make sure you're on the right track. Otherwise, you might wind up in a cornfield or stuck in an industrial part of a strange city. It's the same with your organizational or team goals. Review where you are every so often and see if you need to correct your course.

The rest stops can be monthly or quarterly. Any more frequent and you won't see any pattern. Do them annually, and you could be so far off course you can't get back. Hold meetings in which all the pertinent data is available to everyone, and the clear intent is to review your goals, your progress, assess where you are, figure out where you're falling short, and determine the best way to fix what's not working.

These sessions should be open to any voice; no critique or suggestion is off-limits as long as everybody keeps it professional. But keep them solution based and purposeful—you're not changing things just because someone brought it up.

RUNNING YOUR ROAD MAP SUMMIT

When it's time to get everyone in a room to agree on all of the above, adhere to as many of the following steps as your organization needs to run things smoothly:

STEP 1. Compile your notes from the listen, observe, learn phase into categories, one for each of your core areas of business. Bring in your senior leadership team to review your approach for each core area moving forward. Once that's complete, you're ready to call a meeting with the rest of your management team.

STEP 2. Start the summit by reiterating your organization's values and how they function as the North Star for all your decisions.

STEP 3. Discuss your guiding philosophy for each core area of your business. You may have already talked about this in your one-on-one meetings, but it's worth repeating so everyone can hear it. In my meetings, I discussed my views on areas like setting a clear expectation, training and development, follow-up, and accountability, making them official components of my region's cultural foundation.

STEP 4. Talk at length about where your team, division, or company stands in each of your core business areas at present. Where are you solid? Where are you falling short of your goals or the company's averages?

STEP 5. Present your polished, refined version of your strategic plan—procedures, personnel, customer service protocols, everything relevant. Schedule some breakout sessions to drive home certain points and gain further buy-in, sort of putting the cherry on top. Stick with core areas of the business to avoid getting lost in a thicket of too many topics.

STEP 6. Go over your short- and long-term goals in fine detail. What does success look like, and how will you know when you've gotten there? Your goal is to create an environment that supports your goals—understanding the specifics of each goal is crucial to doing that.

STEP 7. Clearly articulate your expectations for the entire team and for your leaders. Talk with precision about each person's responsibilities. Make sure everyone understands their role in both the immediate situation and the big picture. Remember: people will do more and commit more completely when they fully comprehend what they're doing and why.

STEP 8. If possible, unveil a few surprises for your team, changes or enhancements based on the feedback they gave you in listen, observe, learn that you know they'll appreciate. For example, at my summits, I might roll out a new incentive plan, which always got everybody's attention. I usually removed a few tasks that weren't producing results and were more like busywork.

STEP 9. Announce a challenge, a competition in which your people can participate. This challenge will generally center on the road map's goals and expectations and is designed to create a healthy sense of competitiveness among your team, not to mention helping to build momentum behind the new plan. Challenges in customer service can lead to quick performance improvements that can secure a critical victory for everyone.

STEP 10. Ask all attendees to formally declare their commitment to the details and principles of the road map as well as to each other. Now your road map is locked. Your culture is established or reborn. You're ready for action. As a side note, we always engaged in two critical follow-up items that many managers don't do. First, we made sure our training material matched our new commitments for all levels of employees. Second, we added our key initiatives to our employee reviews, from new hires all the way up to our regional managers. We were very intentional with this. Every action and tactic in your road map must be aligned to create the right behaviors that will lead to the desired outcomes. Awareness is *everything*.

AFTER THE SUMMIT

Once the meetings are over, and everyone has gone back to their offices, the work is just getting started. There are a number of practices that will help ensure that your road map stays at the forefront of everyone's thinking and behavior going forward.

Lather, rinse, repeat. Everyone needs to be on board with your road map, ready to walk the path you've set out. Give everyone on your team every chance to execute the plan repeatedly. For example, to connect with our entry-level staff, we began staging contests to be the manager of the day, creating a shell that the employee would fill out in order to be selected. But all the information involved in the contest was designed to reinforce our most important initiatives, so it created additional buy-in for the road map. People saw that the more they knew about the plan and the more closely they followed it the more likely they were to excel and be rewarded. That made them more likely to take full ownership of plans and make them their own.

Another tool we used to great effect was quarterly meetings with midlevel managers, which gave us an opportunity to drive home the specifics of the methods, processes, and expectations. Your goal should be to *overcommunicate* your material—to talk through each step until all your managers and individual contributors know it backward and forward, and then practice until they can execute as effortlessly as Tony Robbins delivering a motivational speech.

Finally, establish mechanisms to help your high-level people become razor sharp on executing the fundamentals of your plan. In our region, our regional managers ran weekly thirty-minute conference calls every Monday to talk about their observations, and on those calls my area managers would detail their success at keeping their "commitments." At my urging, however, regional managers didn't reveal in advance which area managers would be called on to speak. Sometimes everyone gave an update, but on other calls one area manager might be called on at random. You had to know the material, be on your toes, and be ready to present. Occasionally, we would even have an area manager run the meeting without notice to make sure everyone was ready to lead!

This was about consistently getting better—gaining traction with new goals, behaviors, and ways of doing things. There may be a lot you want to do with your team or organization. But to increase your chances of success, start by making sure your team is executing the fundamentals to perfection. When you prove you can do that, then you can add the best suggestions you've gotten from your team.

Whenever my team and I discussed a task, there was always an exact date and time for delivery. We always had check-in plans, and we were always clear on what they needed to get the job done.

This allowed them to execute at a high level. Trust but verify. How can you let everyone know you will have their back if they stumble? How can you also make it clear you'll be checking up on them should they stray from the chartered course? What are your best practices for keeping tabs on what's happening without seeming like you don't really trust your people?

- Hold people accountable and create momentum. A strong culture is competitive without being cutthroat. I was a stickler for holding people accountable, but in a way that was as empowering and nonthreatening as possible. This approach eventually earned me the nickname the Velvet Hammer. That doesn't mean I would let you get away with anything, because accountability is the mortar in the bricks of any organization or team. But accountability doesn't equal blame. Accountability says, "You made a promise, and I'm holding you to it." It's insisting that people step up and perform at their best. The key to accountability is to break it into two parts. Part one is recognizing and rewarding great performance. Second is what people traditionally think of as accountability—correcting people when they fall short or fail to keep their commitments. The two go together. They are symmetrical. If your team's going to celebrate hitting sales goals, it also needs the ability to look at some people's performance and say, "That's not acceptable." Of course, truly amazing results come when you can get your people to hold each other accountable—and to hold themselves accountable. You do that by creating momentum. There's no reason following a plan for your team or business can't be fun, especially when you consider its ultimate purpose is to make everyone more successful. Get creative making sure your team knows everything about your road map and feels incentivized to give their best. To do that, I used team challenges and quizzes.

•   Challenges. Use one of your first planning meetings to issue a challenge to your team. I'm talking about a competition, usually tied to one or more of the key goals in your road map, with a substantial prize for the winner—which, in this case, was the team. Competition is healthy, and challenges focus employees better than anything else. I wanted them focused on our plan, and this was a way to ensure they knew the goals and were working hard to meet them. Choose a good short-term challenge that can deliver the team an early win, because nothing boosts morale and confidence like an early victory. Make the reward something meaningful, but make the goal meaningful too. Consistently communicate your challenge to your employees. The more people who are aware of it the more word of the challenge will spread. When a team or individual wins, celebrate as a unit, no matter what. Congratulations! You won the contest! You also strengthened belief, communication, trust, pride, and purpose, and helped us grow our winning culture! That's something everyone can celebrate. Be careful of excluding a work group, unless it's intentional. Many of our challenges were meant to include all levels, with slightly different rewards for each position.

•   Quizzes. Sometimes I would issue a well-planned challenge, and then when I went into the field I would find out a lot of my second-level managers had no idea it was going on. That was disappointing. Obviously, the more employees who know about your challenge the more it will improve performance. I didn't want to invest a lot of money and time to have only 10 percent of my team know what was going on. That's how we ended up using quizzes as an individual performance tool. If I wanted a sky-high level of awareness about our challenges and our business road map for the next year, I would rely on the "phone shop" call. I would have my executive assistant call around to all the locations in my region and quiz them on the contest we were running. Whoever answered the phone, they had better know at least some details of the contest and the rewards. That was the branch manager's responsibility. If the employee who answered the phone was able to answer most of the questions correctly, the branch remained eligible for the prize. If not, they were out of the running. A little healthy peer pressure was another useful tool. We had as many as ten separate markets in 24CC, each with its own area manager, and some contests were area specific. We would take advantage of employees' desire not to let their friends down, making it clear if they didn't know their role like the backs of their hands they could end up costing their entire team a prize in the challenge. That made people snap to attention. Your goal is to make sure everyone takes ownership of your plan, understands the methods and deliverables, and follows through consistently.

Do you assume everyone wants to be their best? Then you might need to change how you hold people accountable. What's your plan for helping people whose performance is average to elevate their game? How will you help people willing to learn and who show improvement? What is your strategy for dealing with those who constantly exhibit below-average performance or effort? Accountability demands candor and straight talk, and that's easier when you have a plan.

Culture is a commitment. You always have to be pushing the boulder up the hill. You have to create constant awareness about your plan through field presence, phone calls, training classes, and VIP meetings. That's how you get consistent execution, and consistent execution plus great people equals a winning culture resulting in rewards for everyone.

IN THE REARVIEW MIRROR

- Once you've gathered information and opinions from everyone on your team, it's time to hold a road map summit to communicate your vision to the important players.
- The summit is a time for leadership to gather and commit to the plans and goals for the year ahead.
- The summit should first be guided by your values.
- Your business philosophy, along with the five factors of engagement, will determine how you approach core business activities.
- Your goals and your vision are paramount. Everyone else has already had their say.
- The summit will conclude with the setting of commitments—the actions and strategies you will deploy going forward.
- Run your summit like a fine-tuned machine using the ten key steps.
- Drive home your plan and message with a variety of tools: "lather, rinse, repeat," follow-up, accountability, challenges, quizzes, and more.

CHAPTER 3

CLEAR AWAY OBSTACLES

*Get rid of the impediments to your journey, and create
clarity and simplicity in order to execute efficiently.*

After I became a regional vice president, I was told the prior
leadership team held monthly staff meetings in which they
gathered all the area managers, who ran multiple rental locations, and regional department heads, who ran individual divisions for the entire region, to meet at the regional HQ. These
meetings started at 8:00 a.m. sharp and lasted all day, during
which everyone would present their area and departmental updates.

I'm an early bird, so I showed up at 7:00 a.m. to review the
agenda and grab a cup of coffee. By 7:45 a.m., I said my hellos,
greeted everyone in the room, and took my seat. Eight o'clock
came and went, and nothing happened. While I would normally
grab everyone's attention and get the meeting started, I wanted
to observe how my team would behave without my intervention.
What level of urgency did they have? Since our regional rankings

in many key metrics were among the worst in the company, I was expecting a great deal of urgency, with people showing up on time and anxious to impress. I was disappointed to see the opposite.

By 8:10 a.m., it was clear I needed to get this meeting started. I thanked everyone for coming. Then I asked the room, "Do meetings normally start on time?"

Silence.

You could have heard a pin drop. From there, I made it painfully clear tardiness would no longer be tolerated, unless you had an emergency or family situation. Everything is about *attitude*, *effort*, and *coachability*. Little things matter a lot. No one would get extra credit for showing up on time, I told the team. I looked at timeliness like you would a drive-thru experience at a fast-food chain. When you order your hamburger, you don't get extra credit if it's hot—that's expected.

That wasn't the last time I would have to swing the hammer part of the "velvet hammer" in helping my region become more disciplined and professional. I also observed that my department heads had been discussing some of the same issues for *years*, but nothing had changed. They would spend hours gathering data and preparing reports for these meetings, only to see their work not be used. They were becoming frustrated, and frustration breeds bad habits, excuses, and negativity. Instead, they just complained about problems, leaving area managers feeling like they were being unfairly criticized. Our meetings lacked energy and had a negative tone because people saw them as pointless. In order for the region to be successful, department heads needed the support of the area managers, but they weren't getting it. I dug deeper, looking for the underlying dysfunction, and I quickly found it. The area managers agreed the information was important but were getting so many random emails throughout the month they couldn't manage the information. I had to change the dynamic, and I had to do it immediately. We decided to consolidate some of the reporting and data sent by departments and aligned the timing of the information to match when the area managers would execute their monthly statement reviews. Instead of getting flooded with countless pieces of random info, it was now very purposeful, timely, and easily digestible for an effective statement review.

I also announced to the team that our monthly meetings would now be held twice a year, and the meetings would no longer be about flagging problems and bickering about who was responsible. Instead, they would be about learning and executing the strategic road map for the region. I could almost hear the sighs of relief from my managerial team.

You've created the conditions to listen, observe, and learn everything you can about your team, what it can do, and what it needs. You've got a road map, and you're working on ensuring that everyone knows the plan and is executing it. Now it's time to do something that few leaders ever talk about: getting rid of the complexity and obstacles preventing your team from being exceptional.

ADDING IS EASY, BUT SUBTRACTION IS SMART

Today I sit on a number of boards and partner with organizations I respect. One is Social Venture Partners Connecticut (SVP), a philanthropic network that brings together donors, nonprofits, and social enterprises to have a greater collective impact. We work all over Connecticut, which has the largest *opportunity gap*—the arbitrary circumstances people are born into that they have no control over, such as race, ethnicity, ZIP code, and socioeconomic status, and which determine their opportunities in life—of any other state.

Even in nonprofit organizations, which tend to bring together some of the smartest, most capable people in the country, I see teams making things unnecessarily complicated. When people talk about culture, the message is usually additive. We create programs, write vision statements, do team building, put in place new systems and procedures, and in general, add layers of complexity. There's little talk about clearing things out of the way so people have the bandwidth to follow the cultural road map you've laid out. Remember: clear beats clever!

This "adding is always better" thinking is pervasive in the corporate world. Vivek Gambhir, CEO of boAt Lifestyle, wrote on LinkedIn: "Pruning existing features, structures or regulations is often wiser than bringing in new elements—yet, we naturally associate improvement with addition. When trying to change something for the better, people almost invariably decide to add things. This was the finding of a study by the University of Virginia, published last year in *Nature*. When asked to improve a piece of writing, people added more words. To improve a LEGO construction, they added new pieces. To improve an already crowded travel itinerary, they piled on even more activities. It seems human beings are hardwired for addition, regardless of its relevance or usefulness in a particular situation."[4]

There's nothing wrong with adding new initiatives or procedures

4   Vivek Gambhir, "The Power of Subtraction," LinkedIn, March 3, 2022, accessed April 4, 2022, https://www.linkedin.com/pulse/power-subtraction-vivek-gambhir/?trk=articles_directory.

when they're of value, but often they're not. They're a line item on someone's budget, a favor to a vendor, or the product of an eager executive trying to look decisive. You know you have too much complexity and distraction built into your organization when your listen, observe, learn time reveals

- unnecessary complexity or steps that lead to failure—no traction;
- lack of bandwidth due to overscheduling;
- too much on people's plates, so they feel overwhelmed;
- confusion about what's important—flavor of the month mindset; and
- low productivity.

That's why I worked to keep the culture in my region uncluttered. Communicate clearly and unambiguously. Keep procedures as simple as possible. Get rid of policies and unnecessary activities that don't serve your organization's needs. Question things that nobody has questioned in a while. Don't worry about sacred cows. Remember: activity and productivity are not the same thing.

Let's talk about how to clear obstacles; subtract strategically; and make things leaner, faster, easier, and better for your team so they can stay on the road you've laid out for them. We'll also answer some important questions:

- How do you increase performance by subtracting?
- How do you know what's getting in the way of people executing? For example, do you have six training classes on a topic when you only need two?
- How do you make sure your guidelines, rules, regulations, policies, and procedures aren't muddying your message?

As best-selling author Adam Grant writes: "Overthinking is a problem. Underthinking is a bigger problem. I feel for people who get stuck in analysis paralysis. I worry about people who don't do the analysis in the first place. It's better to embrace the discomfort of doubt than to live with the regret of overconfidence."[5] Simplifying things creates more room for thinking, so let's get to it.

WE TRUST COMPLEXITY EVEN IF WE DON'T KNOW WHY

When you're talking about simplification, it's critical to understand why complexity is introduced in the first place. Often, distrust is the reason organizations engineer complexity into processes and communications. Mike Critelli said in our interview, "People worry that if something is not spelled out, it will not be incorporated. Look at complexity as a symptom of distrust. Government regulations are too detailed because lawmakers distrust the people on the ground to do the right things, so they overengineer regulatory processes and systems."

Unfortunately, human beings tend to favor complexity. One example: contracts. Certainly, you want a binding contract to cover as many contingencies as possible, but the labyrinth of legalese in any contract makes it useless for a layperson to even try to understand it.

---

5   Adam Grant (@AdamMGrant), "Overthinking is a problem. Underthinking is a bigger problem. I feel for people who get stuck in analysis paralysis. I worry about people who don't do the analysis in the first place. It's better to embrace the discomfort of doubt than to live with the regret of overconfidence," Twitter, June 9, 2021, https://twitter.com/adammgrant/status/1402605883734081546? lang=en.

And yet for some reason we sign those documents anyway, reassured that somewhere in the dense language is something that protects us.

There's even a name for this kind of thinking: *complexity bias*, a logical fallacy that leads us to think the more complex something is the more reliable and believable it is. Under complexity bias, if we have a choice between a simple and complex answer to a problem, we're likely to choose the most complex one. We assume that a complex situation needs a complex answer. Sometimes that's true, but not always.

Sometimes simple is best. Unwieldy processes cause delays and increase costs. Unnecessary steps slow things down and frustrate everybody. Simplify where you can. Where you can't, increase information and training. When I became regional VP, I saw that while people were spending a great deal of time at training sessions, they didn't seem to be getting benefits that justified the time away from the office. So I consolidated our trainings to increase efficiency and simplicity. Instead of having employees come to our regional offices for training five times per year, I had them come just three times for ninety minutes longer. They were out of the office less often, putting less of a burden on the folks who had to cover for them, and they learned more because they were mentally and physically fresher.

Less is more. As performance psychologist and author Dr. Jim Loehr has said of world-class athletes, "It wasn't the amount of time that they spent, it was the energy they brought to the time they had, aligned with what the objective was."[6] That's how I thought about my region and my team. I consolidated things like training, and we used our time more efficiently. Employees had to switch mental gears into learning mode less often, but when they did they

---

6   The Tim Ferriss Show, "#490: Dr. Jim Loehr on Mental Toughness, Energy Management, the Power of Journaling, and Olympic Gold Medals," December 28, 2020, accessed September 4, 2021, https://tim.blog/2020/12/28/jim-loehr-2/.

were able to pick up more information. Training results improved.

OFF-RAMP

There's a point where leaders realize that unnecessary complexity has gotten in the way of productivity and happiness, and things have to be simplified. I call that point the horse latitudes. The term comes from the days before steamships, when the world's trade traveled via wind-driven clipper ships.

These vessels would cross the area near the equator known as the doldrums, a region of unpredictable winds and calm areas. Sometimes ships would get stuck in an area with no wind or rain for days or weeks. As the days dragged on, food and water dwindled. In desperation, the crews of ships that carried horses and other livestock would drive the animals over the side and into the sea to make the ship a little lighter and eliminate competition for the limited supplies of freshwater. The poor animals would drown, and this region of the ocean eventually picked up its nickname.

That's a powerful metaphor for getting rid of things that hold you down or keep you from making progress. Every leader of every company eventually sails into the horse latitudes because every company is full of examples of unnecessary complexity that no one questions, because they've been part of the company for such a long time. What procedures or policies that have gone unquestioned for years could you throw over the side and not regret it?

THE DISTRACTION CATCHER

Remember Tim Baxter of Samsung and the Note 7 crisis? At Samsung, Tim was leading a $30 billion business with about twenty-five thousand employees and a multinational culture. Despite that huge challenge, he realized one of his key roles was to be a "cognitive traffic cop" for his direct reports—managing distractions for them, keeping them focused, and directing information they didn't need away from them.

"I tasked myself with creating a North American culture that could live within this broader Samsung culture but have its own sub-identity," he said in our interview. "That meant figuring out when to *amplify* messaging that might be coming from around the globe, when to *buffer* the messaging and how, and when to *pass it along*. To do that, I had to have a pretty good finger on the pulse of the organization."

As a leader, you have the same responsibility to control the flow of information, reduce distractions, and keep your people from getting knocked off course by things that have nothing to do with your goals. What distractions? The list is endless:

- office drama
- customer complaints
- terminations
- financial reports
- useless procedures
- conflicting orders from senior management
- technology breakdowns
- global pandemics

Are you familiar with the spider web–shaped Native American talisman called a dream catcher? The idea is, you hang it near your bed, and the dream catcher catches your bad dreams so you don't experience them. Consider yourself a distraction catcher. Your job is to filter information, rumors, financial news, and more and ensure that none of it bumps your people off the road they're supposed to be on. So you have to choose—note that I've taken Tim Baxter's "amplify, buffer, pass along" method and changed it so it forms an easy-to-remember ABC acronym:

- Amplify. Does the information serve your goals? Is the timing right? Then make sure everybody hears it and hears it well. Repeat as necessary. These would be the initiatives I called my big rock items: important press releases, exciting news, or bad news that's critical to get to all levels of the organization.
- Buffer. Is the information irrelevant, misleading, or confusing and distracting? Correct it, hold it, delay releasing it until you can look into the matter or prepare your team for it, or kill it. At times you will get information that needs to be digested and synthesized. Clarity trumps speed. Get it right and communicate to the appropriate levels. For example, on one occasion, I received a message from HQ strongly encouraging us to open ten stores that would have been open seven days a week. I knew that for our region this was the wrong move. We didn't have the staff, and it would severely impair our ability to execute the plans we had committed to. So I chose to break it into phases until we could build our infrastructure.
- Convey. The timing and message are just right. Send it along to subordinates who will make sure everyone gets a copy. We would call these our sand—not big rock—items, or our "Did You Know?" items a la ESPN. We had our management team use the morning huddles to convey this miscellaneous info.

Be prepared to make the amplify, buffer, convey call with each piece of info that crosses your desk. That's especially true if you're a department head, regional manager, or in some type of leadership position. Like Tim Baxter, you've got your finger on the pulse of things. The bigwigs in the C-suite might not. You know what your people need—and what they *don't* need. Make the call.

DON'T CREATE FEAR

When you start looking for ways to clear the brush and deadwood from your path, it's tempting to just start whacking away. After all, it feels good to throw things away. But now we're back to activity for activity's sake, a backward step. Instead, slow down and think about the impact that discarding a program or procedure could have on your team.

Before I made any drastic changes, I made sure to speak with the people who would be affected by them. Change is difficult under the best of circumstances, and it can be stressful at worst. I wanted to be transparent with anyone whose work might be impacted by discarding distractions or simplifying procedures. I wanted no misunderstandings about why I was doing things.

For example, when I took over my region, I noticed that every task triggered an evaluation or write-up. This created a fearful, negative environment. People felt like they were always on trial. I'm a fan of documentation if you use it to create coachable moments and promote good behavior, but you have to pick your spots. When I came in, I made decisions that were fair, firm, and consistent. With me, you knew you would always be held accountable for

- performance standards in retention, customer service, profits, and growth;

- ethical standards, both personal and business practices; and
- behavior—punctuality, attitude, respect.

The rest of the documentation disappeared, and morale shifted for the better. When you remove complexity, you create a culture around clarity and momentum. As in the sports world, a single play or coaching decision can turn an entire game or season around. Once you set the guidelines for documentation and accountability, however, there's no turning back. You've got to follow through, even if it means terminating people who can't or won't get on board.

Be mindful that the decision you make about simplifying or clearing away deadwood will not please everyone, but when you have trust, your team will follow. As Aesop wisely stated, "Please all and you will please none."[7]

WHAT'S ON THE BUMPER STICKER?

1 PERCENT BETTER

This comes from the book *Atomic Habits* by James Clear. The idea is that you don't need extraordinary changes and extraordinary gains to make your team or company great. You just need to get 1 percent better at a time through small, incremental improvements in clarity, simplicity, efficiency, and productivity. When everyone's on board, you can reach previously unattainable goals. So keep your eyes on the small stuff, and the big stuff will fall in line.

---

[7] Milo Winter, *The Aesop for Children* (Independently published, 2021).

THE MEETING MATRIX

If there's one area of any business that's prone to wasted time and complications, it's meetings. With your meetings, your goal is to be Goldilocks—not too many, not too few, but just right. When I went from monthly staff meetings to two staff meetings per year, I could feel the energy picking up. I told my entire team, "We will not just meet to meet. We will put all our efforts into executing the plan and rewarding those who do it very well." I then requested a listing of every meeting that the organization was presently conducting and its content. Then I started throwing meetings over the side of the boat.

If you want to clear the road ahead for your team to drive fast toward your goals, making your meetings smarter and leaner will help in two ways: First, it will waste less time. Second, it will improve morale and engagement. To help you accomplish that, I've created a tool I call the meeting matrix.

The meeting matrix asks critical questions about your meetings, questions you might not have previously answered. I find that many managers can't justify their meetings very well, saying, "Uh, well, we just have a meeting every Monday morning at ten." But they can't explain *why* they have it. Now it's time to explain why. Run every meeting you've been having through this short series of questions:

- What is the purpose of the meeting?
- How often should we have it?
- How long should it run?
- Is it driving the behaviors and outcomes we want?

Using the meeting matrix, I decided we needed to train our managers to run effective meetings, which I'll discuss in a later chapter. Ask these questions, and pose them to any employee you think will give you straight, useful answers. A few other practices to keep your meetings productive and useful:

- Don't cancel a meeting unless you have no other choice. Canceling meetings is disruptive and disrespectful to people's time. In twenty-six years, I'll bet I canceled 1 percent of my meetings. If I cancel on you at the last minute, it's frustrating. It creates anxiety. You planned part of your day around my meeting, so you couldn't schedule calls, do any work, or make any appointments. Suddenly oops—my bad! Now you're just sitting at your desk, fuming.
- Be predictable. For example, when I announced my retirement, I had to get the message to my team quickly, and I did an uncharacteristic thing: I called an impromptu meeting. My team knew something was up right away. Why? Because normally I would never do that. Meetings should always be scheduled well in advance, and leaders should stick to that schedule.
- Only schedule a meeting for a good reason. Is it really necessary? Could you achieve your goal with a phone call or a Zoom session? When you schedule a meeting, you carve a chunk out of somebody's day, and they don't get that time back.
- Be concise. Keep meetings to the minimum amount of time necessary to achieve the goals of that meeting. A rule of thumb is the shorter the better.

THE BIG THREE

Getting rid of flawed processes and procedures is important, but sometimes tweaking is enough to keep something that could work with the right adjustments. There are three high-impact policies and procedures I'd like to focus on:

1. Performance rankings. Be sure you're ranking the right KPIs that will drive performance and buy-in. But be careful how many items are included in your ranking report. Ranking fourteen items is a sure way to lose energy, team spirit, and belief. I'm a fan of having between four and seven items on a ranking report. It's a number that can be easily understood without complications. Get rid of the rest. Some categories are of greater importance than others. For example, I would double-weight important performance metrics. Also, send out your rankings at the same time on the same day of the week. This will create consistency throughout your system and promote excitement. Our monthly matrix would always drop on the fifteenth of the month, and everyone was eager to see where they ranked because they had worked really hard. I can't tell you how many times during a field visit or in a training class I was asked to confirm that the branch rankings were coming out that day. People were excited to see them. That's when you know your team is getting the message, and things are becoming cultural—when your employees are pestering you to see their performance rankings! Make sure your data is accurate. I always had my executive assistant send a preliminary report to my area managers a few days before the report was due to go out to the branches so they could review

it. Remember what happened to Steve Harvey during the 2015 Miss Universe pageant. He crowned Miss Colombia the winner, and a few minutes later he had to break it to this poor woman that Miss Philippines was the real winner, with hundreds of millions of people watching. Take time to get the data right.

2. Promotion guidelines. From day one, we made sure our employees could review their promotion and advancement status frequently. Culture and trust grow when employees know where they stand on the career ladder. You don't want people thinking they are a lock for the next promotion only to be reminded they don't even qualify. All of a sudden, you have a disengaged employee, and now you've got toxic energy running through your culture. Consider sending out information quarterly or semiannually about who qualifies for advancement by position. This creates ownership, awareness, and a chance to correct a trend that might be headed in the wrong direction. Also, set clear and consistent standards for what qualifies someone to move up, be transparent about them, and make it public when someone makes the jump. Make promotion thresholds fair but firm. Many well-respected companies will require you to rank in the top 25%-50% of a peer group over a select period of time, or have certain benchmarks you must attain in order to qualify for an opportunity. One of the biggest surprises I noticed in my region was the constant movement—mostly due to turnover— and employees being promoted into management after only a few successful months or quarters. While that can be exciting for the person getting the opportunity, it was creating false hope and setting our employees up to fail because they weren't ready for the next step. This policy also encouraged employees to make short-term decisions, hoping for the quick victory that would get them promoted—a dangerous environment for running a business. Everyone began to believe they were due for the promotion because John or Sarah had spent just a few months in the position and had been promoted. It was like an Oprah episode: "You get a promotion, and you get a promotion, and you get a promotion!" To remedy the problem, we came up with a new framework that gave everyone an idea of how long they would need to be at each management position before they became eligible for promotion. This gave everyone a clearer understanding of their career journey and helped them trust the process. Once someone received a promotion into management, I would meet with them to go over their new pay plan. I started that initiative for two reasons: First, I needed a touch point with young managers during an exciting time in their careers. Second, we got a lot of questions about pay, and I learned that how we were communicating the data was rushed, inconsistent, and impersonal. The employee would leave the meeting without clarity. At the end of the meeting, I would ask the employee to explain the pay plan to me so there would be nothing lost in translation. Finally, six months out, we'd have another meeting to review their performance. If they hit the goals we had set, they would receive another bump in pay. This transparency eliminated a lot of distractions and ill will.

3. Rewards. I loved recognizing when my people met or exceeded goals and enjoyed rewarding them for their excellence, so much so that I sometimes paid for their reward out of my own pocket. Make your rewards not only fun but meaningful. For example, I created the **Johnny the Bagger Award** for employees who put our customers first. Johnny the Bagger is a real person, a young man with Down syndrome who got a job as a grocery store bagger. He would find sayings he liked, have his father print them out, and place a "thought of the day" in everyone's grocery bag, in addition to a very sincere, "Thank you for shopping with us." Because of his unfailingly positive attitude and big smile, Johnny's checkout line became the longest line in the store. When one of his co-workers asked a customer if he wanted to switch to a shorter line, the customer proudly said, "No thanks, I'd like to get Johnny's thought of the day." This young man turned a transaction into an interaction and created a memorable experience. The mindset also spread to the entire store. For example, the floral department took all its broken flowers or unused corsages, found elderly women or little girls, and pinned blooms on them.

I fell in love with the story, and it became part of our new-hire training plan on how to create a memorable experience and a special environment. Confirm that your people want your reward. We would mix up our rewards: dinner at my home, a Yankees game, enjoying a beautiful day on a pontoon boat, and some others. Even then, we were flexible. We had monthly dinners for top performers at my home, but initially dinner started at six o'clock, which meant they might not get home until as late as ten. This meant less time with their families, so we listened to the feedback and began the event at three o'clock. Now everyone wanted to be there.

Approach rewards using the same criteria you use for meetings:

- Are we rewarding the right performance?
- Is there buy-in and awareness?
- Are our rewards driving the right behaviors?
- Are they driving the right outcomes?

The purpose of all of this is to keep what works, improve what you can, and get rid of the rest. The goal is to have your team, department, or division running lean, clean, and fast. How will you know if that's happening? Go into the field and get feedback. Constantly review systems and processes and let them go when they no longer serve your purpose. Being clearer and simpler will supercharge your team's motivation, morale, and engagement.

IN THE REARVIEW MIRROR

- Clearing away obstacles to enhance culture is an uncommon approach; most leaders focus on adding.
- Complexity bias makes us trust things that are more complex even if the complexity serves no purpose.
- It's the leader's job to reduce distractions. One way to do this is to be a traffic cop for information, deciding what to amplify, buffer, or convey.
- Keep people informed to avoid creating fear.
- The big three to simplify and clarify: performance rankings, promotion guidelines, and rewards.

CHAPTER 4

CHOOSE YOUR PASSENGERS CAREFULLY

*The people you travel with will make all the difference
in your experience. How do you hire for culture?*

Mike Critelli had a lot of pivotal moments with employees at Pitney Bowes, but one stood out to him when we talked for this book. As an executive corporate staff officer, he was asked to take over the company's financial services division after the previous president had left. Just before taking over, however, Mike received an urgent call from the CEO informing him that a key employee had abruptly left the company to accept a job at Bank of America, then called Nations-Bank. The CEO and Mike both agreed it was a high priority to get this employee back. Thanks to a call from a friend of the ex-employee, who worked for Mike, the ex-employee agreed to call Mike to discuss his willingness to return to Pitney Bowes.

"Coincidentally, he called me on a Monday night, when we were trying to get our two younger children to bed," Mike said in our interview. "They were making a lot of noise, and I apologized and eventually called him back later. To fast-forward, it took a few months, but we got him back."

Naturally, Mike wondered later why this sought-after employee had decided to return. "I asked him, 'What factor was important to you?'" Mike says. "He told me that it was our first conversation. He said, 'When I talked to your predecessor, all too often, the background noise was from a bar. With you, the background noise was children. I wanted a leader who really cared about his family and was home with this family on a Monday night, not in a bar. That's why I left.'"

"Sometimes moments of truth are planned, and sometimes they just happen," Mike concludes, "but they have an outsized importance in creating or sustaining a culture. I pay a lot of attention to moments of truth."

WHO ARE YOU BRINGING ON YOUR ROAD TRIP?

Culture lives or dies based on people. You're on a long journey toward an unknown destination, with big goals and dreams, but the people traveling with you will determine how fast you get where you're going and the kind of shape you're in when you arrive. Do you want to spend years on the road with someone who won't stop changing the radio station or the person who won't stop singing in the car? Or do you want to ride with people who are easy to be with, who make the trip not only more pleasant but contribute something along the way?

In other words, can you hire with your culture in mind? I think you can. You can sometimes train or coach people who don't naturally fit into your culture, but it's easier to hire people for *match*. Not fit, which is the current HR buzzword, but match. To me, fit can be construed as needing to fit into your present culture to excel. I wanted people who would be adaptable and enhance the culture. What's another difference? People who fit your organization might have a needed skill set, have the work ethic, or speak your language. Match is that, but more. New hires who are a good match for your organization have all the qualities of fit but share the values and passion that define your culture. If fit is about the head, match is about the head *and* the heart.

I wanted people who were a match for the way we did things in our region. Hiring the wrong person can be like rolling a live grenade into what you've spent years building. In my experience, people tend to hire for job skills but fire for behaviors, so recruitment was one of the first aspects of the region I revamped, top to bottom, from the process to the questions to the people involved.

I started with our talent acquisition team, which, like many organizations, search the many recruiting sites, attend a number of job fairs, and reach out to college campuses, looking for a diverse group of future employees. For example, talent acquisition might bring in a manager trainee candidate who appeared to check the basic boxes, and if they felt that person had the capacity to do the job and could give good answers to good questions, the prospective hire would go to the area manager. That person would focus on competencies like leadership, sales, critical thinking, communication style, and problem solving. They would use the person's résumé and ask behavioral interview questions, like, "Tell me about the last time you had an interaction with a salesperson," or, "Tell me what you did the last time you dealt with an irate customer."

We would rank this candidate, and if they looked like a potentially good match for a leadership position in 24CC, they would get to me. I only saw managerial candidates who were the cream of the crop.

We developed this stringent screening process out of necessity. Traditionally, I would hold a lunch for our new hires, usually a few weeks after they started their careers. That was my chance to learn about them. We would go around the table—there were usually three or four employees at each lunch—and each person would share a few details about themselves—siblings, where they grew up, hobbies, that sort of thing. I would also open up the floor to any questions they wanted to ask me. It was a fairly relaxed setting.

At one particular lunch, I had an unusually large group, and I was excited to learn about our future stars. But as I listened to them, I couldn't believe what I was hearing. Most seemed more interested in complaining about the company than learning about each other. Within three months, seven of the eight had resigned. That lunch was the catalyst for a new interview process.

Many leaders insist they don't have time to be involved in hiring. Take it from me: make the time. Hiring is a skill, and it takes practice to understand the right questions to ask, how to evaluate responses, and how to recognize someone who suits your culture, not to mention ensuring you're well educated so no one is falling victim to unconscious biases in the selection process. Coincidentally, after fine-tuning our interview process, hiring and retention efforts in our region evolved into some of the best in the company and stayed that way for more than a decade.

LOOKING FOR "MATCH"

When I did finally sit down with a managerial candidate, I was looking for match. How do you spot that? For me, it started with the opening line of the interview, in which I would give the candidate a thirty-second version of what they could expect. I wanted them to understand that we were interviewing each other to determine if we were a good match. This allowed the candidate to be as authentic as possible during a potentially nerve-racking interview process. A good interviewer can pull things from people about their qualities and characteristics that they might not normally reveal.

Next, I would ask the candidate to "tell me your story." Why? I wanted the candidate to lead the conversation without me saying a word. The moment you start asking questions about sales, service, or their leadership, it gives a signal of what's important to you and your company. I wanted to understand their story—who they were and what was important to them—without them feeling guided. They didn't realize it, but this was one of the most important questions I would use to evaluate them.

First impressions mattered a great deal to me too. In those few minutes, I would often know whether I was going to hire this person or not. I was also looking for consistent themes throughout the interview based on their opening story. Again, I wanted them to relax so I could get an authentic sense of their personality and communication style, and what better way than to have them talk about themselves? I guess you could say this was the "velvet" part of the velvet hammer.

After this opening, I would dig into questions to try and uncover their why, what, and who. Again, I wanted their thoughts, words, and actions to come unprovoked. No free passes here. Why did business intrigue them? What got them excited about running their own business? What were their bigger goals? Who were their mentors or role models? Along the way, I'd take mental notes about their character, confidence, and poise. Was 24CC a place where they could be successful? That mattered more than their educational background because I would interview people with a variety of college majors, not just business. You can train smart people to be competent in important skills.

Bottom line: attitude and character often trump skills. Another key piece of the interview process was finding out how candidates responded to being pushed into a corner, and if they would stay committed to what they believed in. I would try to nudge the candidate just a little outside their comfort zone. I guess you could say this was a bit of the "hammer." For example, I might ask a question and take the opposing side.

I might ask, "Do you hate to fail or love to succeed?" There is no right answer, but I can see how they work their way through a situation, demonstrate their character, and how composed they are, and can better understand their thought process.

In every interview, the last thing I said was always, "It's important that this is a great match. After you leave, I want you to go talk to a mentor and go over all the important details in order to make a great career decision. Then ask yourself, 'Is this a place I could see myself being for the long term?'" My goal was to hire long-timers who had the vision to see our potential. Those are the people I wanted to drive with.

OFF-RAMP

People tend to be at their best when they're on a job interview, and

I wanted to see everyone's true character. So I had a trick up my sleeve when I was interviewing managerial candidates.

I would ask my HR manager or executive assistant to introduce themselves to the candidate in the lobby. They would not give their title, but instead would shake hands and say, "Hey, I'm Jen, nice to meet you," so the candidate would have no idea who they were. If the candidate came across as dismissive, snobby, or hostile to this person they didn't know, it didn't necessarily mean they were out of the running, but it was a strike against them. After all, if they can't treat my team right, how are they going to treat a customer or another employee?

The story has two morals: First, treat everyone with respect. Second, all's fair in determining if someone belongs in your culture.

YOU WANT THE STEAL OF THE DRAFT

Hiring to match a painstakingly calibrated corporate culture is like drafting a pro athlete. You're looking for people with world-class talent, but there are only so many of those, and *everybody* wants them. So you're looking for something else too: the hidden gems, the steals. Anyone can pick people with extraordinary talent. They stand out. It's harder to spot the diamonds in the rough—the quiet talents with guts and grit who, with the right coaching and some hard work, could be just as great as the first-round picks, and maybe better. Someone like Tom Brady, who was the sixth QB taken in the 2000 NFL draft and the 199th pick, only to become the greatest QB of all time.

I spoke with Ted Fleming, then head of talent development for CVS Health, which has more than three hundred thousand employees. He thinks the same way about hiring. "I certainly think people can train and develop," he said in our interview. "But when I look at problems in middle management and the executive level, and if I do a root cause analysis, there was usually an issue in the hiring. They ignored a red flag. Training and development helps, the culture helps, but you've got to start with something. There has to be a footing under the foundation you are trying to build."

"I might want people who have an enterprising mindset, who are good leaders, who can build high-performing teams, and who can think strategically. They don't have to be good at all those things, but they do have to *want* to be good at them," Ted concludes. "I can teach you all sorts of things, but I can't teach you to care. If you don't care about our customers, and you don't care about your coworkers, I can't help you."

In any field, you're looking for recruits with a "high ceiling," people with the potential to learn and grow in their role and to surpass their role. That's what I looked for. I also knew there were certain qualities that would give any individual a better chance of being successful on our team. Could they communicate with clarity and empathy? Were they coachable and adaptable? Did their life experience suggest they were resilient? University of Pennsylvania psychologist Angela Duckworth, best-selling author of *Grit*, says, "It's resilience, not IQ, that is the best predictor of success."[8]

Is your recruit tough? Do they have the belief in themselves to get up after they get knocked down and to keep pushing forward after a failure? Even the best and brightest fail. Even Simone Biles, arguably one of the best gymnasts ever, falls off the balance beam once in a while. Resilience is especially important at the entry level

8   Angela Duckworth, *Grit: The Power of Passion and Perseverance* (New York: Scribner, 2016).

because a new recruit might be bounced around between all sorts of different jobs. All the talent in the world is useless if someone you're counting on has a meltdown because you've asked them to do something that's outside their comfort zone.

THE INTERVIEW PROCESS

In a tough hiring environment, the idea of hiring for cultural match and character rather than checkboxes on a résumé is popular. I talked with David Pachter, cofounder of JumpCrew, a Nashville-based outsourced sales company, and he told me that when his company was growing exponentially before COVID-19 hit he had no qualms about bringing in people with no sales background.

"When we had our first hiring spree, the first one hundred folks we hired for client-facing positions had no sales experience. We didn't want the baggage associated with someone having learned sales a different way," David said in our interview. "We knew that if we hired one hundred experienced salespeople, they would bring a hundred different sales cultures with them, and ninety-five of those would be incompatible with our culture."

"We specifically hired folks who didn't have sales training, knowing that we'd need to provide a tremendous amount of extra hand-holding and support for them to become professional B2B sales folks," David concludes. "But we hired with that specific cultural mindset, and in fact I think we ended up with half a dozen folks from Enterprise."

With a tight labor market, interviewing for match is more important than ever. If you make a bad hire, you can't simply call one of your other candidates. They've probably already gotten jobs. You need a smart, effective interview process. Consider these factors for a smart and effective interview process:

- Know your questions in advance. I had a go-to tool kit of questions that told me if a candidate was strong or weak in the traits that were important to me, like communication, empathy, and coachability. I assume you know the traits that are important to your organization, so be sure you have your own questions ready to be brought out after the niceties and small talk are over.
- Watch for "tells." In poker, a "tell" is a mannerism or behavior that tells an opposing player something about you. Maybe your eye twitches when you're bluffing, and good players will use this information to beat you. Job candidates have tells that will give you insight into who they are. After conducting thousands of hiring interviews, I can tell you that a consistent "tell" is when someone uses empty buzzwords continuously. For example, they might say, "I am an overachiever," or, "I have strong time management skills," but they are unable to provide good examples of their exceptional abilities. To me, one of the biggest tells is when the candidate doesn't answer the questions asked. This usually meant they either weren't actively listening or were trying to ad lib because they couldn't support their claims. Lastly, when someone couldn't give me an example of the last time they failed at something or just blamed others for their failure, that was a red flag. No prima donnas allowed! You need to take ownership.
- Know what someone with a "high ceiling" looks like. Game-changing talent is rare, but people with potential aren't. Be clear on which is which, as the type of person you need will be different from the kind of employee we looked to hire. Can you recognize someone who might not have great natural gifts

but who's scrappy, coachable, resilient, and of high integrity? Someone with high emotional intelligence and a knack for cognitive diversity? Giving the applicant situational questions, such as, "What would you do if your best employees were crossing an ethical line?" To me, the formula for a high-ceiling employee is when inner drive meets coachability, character, and consistency.

• Ask clarifying questions. By asking follow-up questions, you will avoid making gut-feeling hires, which rarely works out. Too many interviewers ask a question without digging in, assuming they know what the candidate was referencing. Be disciplined and ask further questions so you can understand the applicant's thought process. For example, a candidate says, "Sales is challenging." You respond with, "What did you mean by that?" Are they making excuses because they fear they won't be able to sell? Someone might say, "I hear you work long hours here," and the interviewer might assume they're afraid of hard work. Again, a follow-up question would clarify.

• Know your red flags. Because candidates only came to me after passing two other interviews, I didn't sit down with a lot of people who had glaring weaknesses. But sometimes I saw warning signs that this candidate might not be a good match. Inconsistencies on the résumé were one. Another was oversharing too much personal information. We all have events in our lives that have shaped our behaviors, but just make sure you have boundaries. What would they be sharing after a month or a year on the job? Will they mention our conversation to someone else? If the candidate had no questions for me at the end of the interview, that was a big red flag. Really? I'm asking you to make a long-term commitment, and you don't want to know anything? I liked inquisitive people who asked challenging questions. By the way, if someone who sent up red flags made it to my office, I would have a coachable moment with the area manager who had interviewed the candidate and passed them up the chain to me. I wanted that to happen as infrequently as possible.

• Be mindful of both verbal and nonverbal cues. Everything I did during the interview I did to evaluate the candidate. When I asked questions about their accomplishments, I didn't just listen to what they said in reply but how they said it so I could gauge their comfort level and confidence. Does their body language support their message? Did they have the right instincts of when to expand upon an answer and when to state and wait? Verbal and nonverbal cues are equally important.

• Keep the candidate informed. Let the candidate know what's next and when they'll hear from you. If they hear good news, what comes after that? The better your communication, the more stars you're apt to land in a tight labor market. New hires earned a ticket to Club Elite, our monthly awards banquet, to feel the special culture. We wanted them to feel that 24CC was their "home court," where the energy was contagious.

⬆ ROADSIDE ATTRACTION

Many interviewers, especially in sales, fall into the trap of hiring the extroverted candidate who can work the room and shows up with lots of energy while dismissing the introvert who might be just as qualified but just not as charismatic. That's natural. We all love a stirring speech, but don't be seduced by someone who might be persuasive but lacks the skills or substance your team deserves. Some of my best salespeople were introverts.

I found a real-life example of this when hiring a senior-level employee. There were several openings, and we did a round-robin interview process with a neighboring region. My counterpart fell in love with a candidate who could talk the talk. I went for the candidate who was more low-key but laser sharp. Interestingly enough, one employee became an officer of the company, and the other decided to pursue other opportunities a few years later. I am sure you can guess who was fortunate to make the right hiring decision.

Salespeople aren't always extroverts, and IT professionals aren't always introverts. Interview for character and match, and avoid stereotyping. You might be pleasantly surprised.

THE END

Terminations need to be handled delicately, and I'm not just talking about avoiding legal action. Someone might not click with your company culture but could still be extremely popular or someone that a department has learned to rely on. Letting them go in the wrong way could cause resentment or damage the trust in your culture—not to mention your personal brand—so it's important to tread carefully.

My key principles about letting someone go:

- Be empathetic but succinct. Just get to the facts of why they're getting let go, but you must ensure the person delivering the news understands the enormity of the situation and demonstrates empathy. In most cases, this should not be a surprise— furloughed or laid-off employees would be a potential exception. If I have to terminate someone, progressive management means they should have been well aware there was a problem.

• Walk them through the process. Depending on the circumstance, some employees might be receiving a severance package, extended insurance benefits, or an outplacement service to assist with a new job. Be very clear about their particular situation.

• Be kind. "Thank you for the last three years. I'm sorry it had to end this way, but I wish you the best."

• Be clear with your leaders. Let them know why this person was let go so they know how to answer questions if or when someone approaches them. Depending on the level of employee, you might need to communicate to the entire team. There is nothing worse than hearing about a termination at the water cooler or worse yet from the terminated employee. That way, you control the messaging. The process of terminating someone should be just as predictable and purposeful as the process of hiring.

• In-person versus virtual meeting. While not always logistically possible, it's always better to deliver the bad news in person. Here's an example of how not to do it: Vishal Garg, the CEO of Better.com, learned the hard way during a Zoom call in which he unceremoniously fired nine hundred employees—the equivalent of 9 percent of his workforce—one day after receiving a $750 million cash infusion from its funders. Not to mention, Garg admitted to making berating comments on a social media site, stating that employees were stealing from customers and working two-hour days. The entire situation was mishandled, and their brand was damaged. Shortly after the debacle, Garg took a leave of absence.[9]

---

9   Jason Aten, "The CEO Who Fired 900 Employees on a Zoom Call Is Out. It's a Tragic Example of How Not to Manage People," Inc., December 14, 2021, accessed April 4, 2022, https://www.inc.com/jason-aten/the-ceo-who-fired-900-employees-on-a-zoom-call-is-out-its-a-tragic-example-of-how-not-to-manage-people.html.

The clear answer is, "Yes, you can hire for culture." Do it carefully and thoughtfully, keeping in mind your destination and the other passengers in the car with you. Most of all, remember that when you were hired by your organization, you probably didn't check every one of their "ideal employee" boxes. They took a chance on you anyway. Be open to doing the same. You never know when the "wrong" person will turn out to be the right choice.

IN THE REARVIEW MIRROR

- Yes, you can hire for culture.
- Your people are your passengers on this road trip toward success.
- You're looking for "match," not "fit."
- The goal is to find talent others have missed—people with a "high ceiling," or tremendous untapped potential.
- Construct interview questions carefully, looking for "tells" and red flags and asking clarifying questions.
- Handle termination with as much care and finesse as hiring.

CHAPTER 5

TRAIN YOUR PEOPLE TO BE CULTURE CARRIERS

Empower through training and development; share your knowledge and wisdom as you travel so your people can carry your culture when you're not on the road with them.

F rances Frei has said, "Leadership, at its core, is about making other people better as a result of your presence—and making sure that the impact lasts in your absence."[10] That's the essence of culture, a way of thinking and behaving that persists without having to be enforced. That only happens through focused, effective training.

Training is your most powerful tool for igniting and sustaining a strong culture. That seems counterintuitive, doesn't it? Culture

---

10   Frances Frei and Anne Morriss, *Unleashed: The Unapologetic Leader's Guide to Empowering Everyone Around You* (Boston: Harvard Business Press, 2020).

often seems to be something abstract, something that arises from things like brand, spirit, values, and personality. Those are aspects of culture. But remember: at its heart, culture is about behaviors and values. Training ensures that your people have what they need to do things the right way and achieve desired goals.

Take another look at the five factors of employee engagement. Many of them have a focus on training:

1. A strong relationship with the manager.

2. Clear communication of expectations and goals.

3. The right materials, equipment, and information to achieve the desired outcome.

4. Management that encourages personal and professional development.

5. A system in which top performance is recognized.

Those factors were consistently my best tools for keeping my team feeling connected, motivated, enthusiastic, and ambitious about the work we were doing. Effective training programs communicate expectations and goals, give people the information they need to get the job done, and encourage growth.

But some leaders and organizations don't see that their training has to evolve with the business and its people. You can't offer the same training curriculum for ten years in a row. It will become obsolete, and you'll lose your audience. But that's precisely what some organizations do. They get set in their ways or beholden to the same vendor, and the training *fossilizes*. You have to keep your finger on the pulse of your division or your department or your company, watch what's changing, listen to your people, and let that information drive how and when your training material changes.

Training and directives used to come from the top down. Senior executives set goals, managers implemented them, and the individual contributors did the work. But that has changed. Today collaboration has become a *big deal*, especially with millennials. We quickly learned that the younger generation doesn't want to be siloed. They want to collaborate, learn, and contribute, which I admire. That meant we had to change how we trained people.

Also, we were always reviewing our training material and trying to make it more effective. This was an all-hands-on-deck affair as department heads and area and regional managers reviewed material to ensure that training provided the coaching and guidance needed to execute our road map at an elite level. If some training needed updating due to technology advancements or new product rollouts, we ensured that our materials supported all new initiatives. Changes for one level of employee found their way into the training for every level because everyone had to be on the same page. We reviewed all our training and made further tweaks or enhancements twice a year.

I also learned that to keep training evolving you can't stay in your office. You need to be in the field, learning what's going on and getting feedback on what your people need to execute your initiatives at a high level. This is a part of the listen, observe, learn process. My senior leaders would go to our stores and identify areas of opportunity that might require more training.

We had "octopus hands," always looking at ways to tighten up or enhance training. We didn't change things lightly, because that invites confusion and doubt. But by always polishing and having up-to-date content in our training programs, we kept things fresh, relevant, and easy to execute in order to produce elite results.

OFF-RAMP

When you care about helping your people grow and advance, it often creates a lasting bond. When you got promoted to area manager, we would throw you a roast—bring in friends, tell funny work stories about you, that sort of thing. Well, there was an individual who had been on my team, and there had been some trust issues with him. I wish I had found a way to be a better mentor to him. But when he got up to speak, he brought me on stage, and he was crying. He said, "It wasn't always perfect, but I am who I am because of you, Eric."

It was the expression of gratitude from employees that mattered to me. Those are the moments when you know people respected the knowledge you helped them gain and the hard work you inspired them to stick with, and that feels good. To this day, there are some former employees who I trained who call themselves the "Rolling Stones." They've moved on to bigger and better things, but it's good to know there are so many people out there who feel good about their experience and my leadership.

A TRAINING CULTURE

There are many ways to help your people learn:

- On-the-job (OTJ) training. This can occur at the work site, although with so many people working remotely, OTJ training can also happen via a distance learning platform. In either case, it will usually feature a blend of intensive training followed by real-time application.

• One-to-one coaching, or a day in the field. This is informal but amazingly effective. There are hundreds of decisions made every day at a business, and if you're not training at the local level you are losing hundreds of coachable moments. Managers or trainers should be available to coach and guide employees in real time, especially when they're struggling with things like technology, difficult customers, or complex procedures.

• Morning and midmorning huddles. First thing in the morning, managers should meet with employees to go over themed topics, which can vary by the day—for instance, sales, service, and costs—and discuss roles and responsibilities for the day. Midmorning huddles give managers a chance to gather their team and go over the early successes or opportunities they've witnessed.

We would balance on-the-job training with one-on-one training sessions. I would have rotating visits with my regional managers, area managers, and department heads, and my regional managers would have rotating visits with the area managers, branch managers, and assistant branch managers. In all those visits, we would constantly monitor how our team was executing on our commitments and provide coaching, guidance, or a high five to create a consistent experience for our team.

This was more lather, rinse, repeat, but nobody got tired of it, because we all knew it was making us better. As our numbers improved, and the training yielded visible results, everyone became even more committed. Branch managers, training with their local team, would do the same kinds of things. We used training, repetition, and practice to create a cloak of invincibility around 24CC.

As researcher George Bray writes: "Genetics loads the gun, but the environment pulls the trigger."[11] We knew if we took talented people and gave them an environment in which they could learn and excel the entire region would benefit. We built a professional development master's degree for the rental car industry.

Many organizations mix it up and get creative in training and development. Walmart was looking for a way to reduce the cost that comes with injuries, risks, and accidents. They found an e-learning company with a microlearning platform that provided employees with the training they needed to ensure workplace safety. Apparel company Bonobos offers hyperfocused courses, like "Managing for Success," to teach management skills; "Fit for Success" to teach performance management training; and "How to Manage Up Well" to teach associate-level employees to navigate their relationships with senior employees. Beauty giant L'Oréal developed the world's first employee onboarding app to help new employees understand, decode, and master their company culture. Ten thousand new hires use the app, which is available in eleven languages, each year.

The point is not to have just training programs but a *training culture*. Training culture goes beyond training programs to breed an environment in which the entire organization is suffused with enthusiasm for learning, coaching, asking hard questions, and problem-solving. For example, my team used an approach called SOS— show, observe, and shape. Show someone how to do something, then observe them doing it, and then shape the behavior you just witnessed. In an optimal training culture, OTJ training ideas that work would even be archived in a central database so anyone could

---

11   George A. Bray, *Contemporary Diagnosis and Management of Obesity and the Metabolic Syndrome* (Newton, PA: Handbooks in Health Care, 1998).

access and use them while also being incorporated into the next version of training.

In a training culture, learning occurs every day in every environment, not just at certain locations and at predetermined times. I would always ask my team, "What did you learn today?" I wanted all of us to truly think about the work we were doing and understand why we were doing it, not just how. That's "training on purpose." That's how employees can step back and see all the knowledge they've acquired, improving awareness and buy-in.

CULTURE CARRIERS

Creative, meaningful training is your opportunity to create what Claude Silver, Chief Heart Officer at digital branding agency VaynerMedia—and recently ranked by Engagedly as one of the top one hundred HR influencers—calls culture carriers. Those are people who not only champion your culture but carry it with them at all times by how they behave, what they say, and how their values align with the corporate culture. They make your culture contagious by speaking it, living it, and believing it.

Culture carriers not only know your culture but love it and take pride in it. They ensure that even when you're not present at a specific location the culture you've created is visible. They are your resources for scaling your culture—expanding it into new areas and sharing it with new groups. They're the "Mini Me" versions of you who you'd like to seed throughout the organization, and you start to find and encourage them through meetings like these, as Claude explained when I spoke with her.

Claude told me that she uses culture carriers to scale the

company even though she can't possibly meet with all one thousand employees in person. With strong culture carriers, she doesn't have to. They're her proxies, going out into the world wearing the VaynerMedia heart on their sleeves and engaging, hoping to attract like-minded spirits. Culture carriers are like the informal leaders in a sports clubhouse or locker room. They show everyone by example how things are supposed to be done.

Culture carriers are typically enthusiastic, charismatic employees who believe in the company and share its values but are also strong communicators. Remember Ted Fleming, who was the head of talent development for CVS Health? I spoke with Ted about culture carriers, and he told me the company trains people to sow cultural "seeds" throughout the organization.

"We've actually trained two hundred and fifty cultural ambassadors," he said in our interview. "If we're coming out with a new community service program or rolling out a new training, these are people we can call and get together to get their thoughts on how they think it will play out with their constituent groups."

CVS doesn't stop there. "We have cultural training for new hire onboarding," Ted adds. "We also do training based on what we call 'work behaviors.' We have thirteen work behaviors that are the foundation of our culture and are tied to our five values, and there's a required training on that. We will also do training for leaders on culture and what their responsibility is. We do lots of training on how your thinking drives behaviors, which drive results."

In the end, your goal is to train your own people to be culture carriers. You can nurture them through leading by example but also by training them relentlessly in your organization's values, methods, and expectations. You'll have the greatest success implementing your road map and getting everyone on board when you have small groups or units assisting in the delivery of that plan. Culture carriers serve that goal.

MENTORING

After I joined the company right out of college, it didn't take me long to see it was a one-of-a-kind place. Within six months, I became a management assistant and met my mentor, John. He took me under his wing, and I really started to blossom. Instead of just having me do things, he explained why I should do them. We talked, I asked questions, and he answered them clearly and completely. Near the one-year mark, I became an assistant manager, the person in charge of the minute-to-minute operations, and I went back to run the original retail location where I had been hired. John's mentoring gets a lot of the credit for my quick advancement.

Mentoring even made me change how I signed my name. I had been with the company for five or six months, and I noticed how my branch manager signed his name. It looked cool, and I looked up to him, so I started signing my name the same way. To this day, I write my signature the same way. That's transformative. I was fortunate to work alongside people of great influence and wisdom, who allowed me to take certain trainings and ideas, make them my own, turn them loose, and see what happened. They trusted me, and I trusted them. Because of that, I knew I wanted to earn the trust of the people I led.

If you want to train your people to embrace and grow a winning culture, institute a mentoring program. In fact, you're crazy if you don't have one. What better way is there to pass on critical knowledge and cultural values than to have a higher-level employee personally guide a lower-level employee through the opportunities and challenges that lie ahead?

There are several ways to mentor. You can have a formal mentor program, in which you pair young employees with experienced employees. You can also run a group mentor program, in which one mentor meets with several mentees to discuss important topics and answer questions. Not only does this allow the employees to expand their network but it also gives senior individual contributors experience as leaders. In my region, everyone at the manager level and above participated in the mentor program and was assigned new recruits to mentor, which put an exclamation point on the serious nature of the mentoring program.

Mentees would deliver monthly reports on their relationships with their mentors. They would answer questions like, "Have you had regular contact with your mentor this month?" and "What guidance did your mentor give you this month?" and go over in detail what they and their mentor talked about and worked on. In this way, we selected our mentor and mentee of the month, which I talk about below. We also held our mentors accountable and would remove mentors from the program if they failed to take it seriously.

It's essential that you have small groups or units within your organization that can assist with the development of your culture. The more voices and opinions involved, the stronger your culture. The organization is like a pack of animals in the wild. If there's no mingling with other packs, there's too much inbreeding, which leads to genetic defects and disease. Crossbreeding means genetic diversity and a stronger population. You want mentored teams with their own ideas speaking up and speaking out.

THINK TANK

The think tank program, which I created in my region, was one way we nurtured culture carriers with mentoring. Each year, I would assemble a select group of high-potential and high-commitment managers to spend time with me throughout the year. We would meet every other month, and in order to be selected you had to be voted in by your peers and be in good standing in terms of performance. I also ensured that the group included people who represented diversity of culture, gender, race, and thought. To stay in the think tank, you had to meet stringent performance standards throughout the year. The employees chosen usually stayed on the team for at least a year, and once their rotation was over we would bring in replacements.

My think tank members got some group coaching on varied topics to help them up their game. But mostly I wanted them to assist in implementing the strategies our region needed to perform at the highest level in the core areas of our business. Being on my think tank was a big responsibility.

I encouraged members of the think tank to challenge my ideas. I wanted polite disagreements on important topics, not sycophants. The point of mentoring was to empower everyone to think outside the box, challenge the status quo, and ask questions I might not know the answers to. Typically, those employees were closest to the field, and I needed their reality to counterbalance my perception.

The think tank experiment was a huge success. Our mentored group came up with a number of key strategies that the region embraced, and they helped us become one of the most successful regions in the company. These young managers developed the agenda ahead of our meetings and helped with the communication of all initiatives, making them another voice for our region. They became unparalleled culture carriers. The only thing I really did was recap our meetings to the region's senior leadership so they knew in advance about new strategies that might be coming down the pike. Our young stars did the rest of the work.

Before long, everyone wanted to be a part of the think tank. A new employee once reached out to me after one of our training classes and asked, "How do I get on the think tank?" When your people are asking about doing *more* work, you're onto something. These mentored groups became one of our region's calling cards, and all of a sudden, neighboring regions started to create their own leadership groups.

Mentoring became so important that we started awarding a mentor and mentee of the month. They got invited to a special dinner every other month at my house, where my wife and I treated everyone like a very special guest, which they were.

One more thing: You've got to train people to be mentors. It's not an inborn skill, and not everyone can do it. Look for senior employees who are good listeners, enjoy teaching, have a strong personal brand, can take their ego out of situations, and enjoy sharing what they know. Those are your mentors. Also, encourage people to move beyond having just one or two mentors. I asked my employees to seek out other mentors after about six months, in effect creating their own personal boards of advisors. That got them out of their comfort zone and opened them up to new opinions and ideas. Don't be afraid to invert the concept, too: try reverse mentoring, which is a type of mentorship that allows junior-level employees from underrepresented groups to be paired with senior-level leaders and voice their perspective about some of the opportunities or challenges they may face.

THE "STAY INTERVIEW"

My HR manager and I had one more cultural training and development trick up our sleeves. Every month she would meet with up to ten employees for what we called "stay interviews." A stay interview was a personal visit to ask employees important questions: Were they aware of our regional commitments? Were their training time lines up-to-date? How well were we living up to the expectations we set when they were hired? This turned out to be a wonderful way to get a pulse on the business from someone besides myself. Stay interviews provide a unique opportunity to reassess how much of your culture needs a jumpstart and create a strong relationship with a department head while showing authenticity and approachability.

My HR manager and senior leadership would review all the answers monthly to get a sense of our team's culture. To encourage the right training behaviors, my HR manager would track which branches were seeing more employees advance. We wanted to recognize people who were moving into a leadership role, underscoring the importance of creating a "pay it forward" mindset.

 # ROADSIDE ATTRACTION

Mentoring humanizes everyone because it tells people what they don't know. That's huge. I always wanted the people on my team to see that I was a human being and not just the guy in a suit they saw at the office. So I let them know that not only do I love rap but I can talk about it with authority. They would say, "Nuh-uh, you? Stone, I thought you were, like, an opera guy." Nope, I know the entire Rick Ross catalog and can freestyle—well, let's not go that far. They didn't realize I'd played college baseball until I told them, because they couldn't see me as an athlete. Then we'd play basketball or Wiffle ball, and they would say, "Yo, Stone's got some game." I became more relatable and more real through these exchanges.

NOBODY TRAINS ON THIS STUFF, BUT THEY SHOULD

I've said that we trained our mentors, but I didn't stop there. If culture boils down to behaviors and values, then your people have to know how to carry out important behaviors at a high level for your culture to flourish. That's why we would train our people on behavioral skills that most organizations don't even think about training people on. I suggest you do the same.

SKILL 1: Time management. What's one of the most common employee complaints? "I don't have enough time." The truth is, there is usually plenty of time, but the million-dollar question is: How are your people utilizing their time? When you struggle with time management, it creates stress, frustration, and anxiety. When you're overwhelmed, you become unproductive, often going into a downward spiral. In business, this is a surefire way to wind up with people who are burned out and disengaged.

My theory was that if we could train our team in a few best practices for time management they would have the tools and skills to better execute their roles and responsibilities. This would build their personal success, which would build a winning culture. If they wanted, they could even apply these techniques at home. This was also my way of ensuring that health and wellness became a positive side effect of this training.

SCHEDULE. Are we scheduling our employees to match both the business needs and their personal needs? One of the biggest reasons we struggled getting things accomplished was that when we needed the employees to handle the flow of business they weren't there. We were scheduling them according to what they wanted first instead of what was best for the customer. This caused us to fall behind and created more work for our team in critical times. So we empowered our team to review key transaction data for each day of the week and then focused on which hours in the day were busiest. Based on the trends, they would submit an employee schedule for the following month by the twenty-fifth of the month to ensure we were properly staffed and able to assist our customers. We called this "scheduling with precision." Creating a well-thought-out schedule in advance also allows your employees to plan their own time off, which is important when they're trying to balance both work and home life.

PRIORITIZE. I had my managers prioritize everything they needed to accomplish in a typical month. To each, they attached a time commitment. For example, making sales calls might take twenty-plus hours in a month. Interestingly, there were really only five to seven items that drove the majority of the performance. That's the old Pareto principle in action: 80 percent of the effects come from 20 percent of the causes. We scheduled these assignments in advance and ensured no one ever missed them. They became our staple items—our big rock items. After we implemented our time-saving strategy, we had our people take the hours they worked in a month and subtract the time it took to complete their tasks. They were pleasantly surprised to see there was a good amount of time left to execute their job.

THE FOUR Ds. When faced with a time-consuming task, fall back on one of the four Ds:

- Do—do it yourself.
- Delegate—pass the task on to someone else, along with clear instructions. If you delegate, be sure the person has the skills and knowledge to handle the assignment, set a definitive due date, schedule follow-up to make sure things are done right and on deadline, and be sure the person you're delegating to knows the consequences of completing or not completing the assignment.
- Defer—is the need immediate? Is the urgency real? If not, then reschedule this task for another window, when you have more time.
- Delete—if the task is irrelevant, unproductive, or a waste of time, kill it. One example is the "nice to know but not need to know" email.

SIMPLIFY. Get rid of any duplication or unnecessary items that don't drive the right behaviors.

WIN THE MOMENT. Every branch had a sheet that listed daily responsibilities—and whose roles coincided with which task—and suggested a few best practices on how to "win the moment." By winning the moments, you inevitably start winning the day, week, and month. In football, they break everything down by the play. Win each play, and you win the series, then the drive, and then the game.

SKILL 2: How to lead. Leaders are made, not born. I was in a strategy session with my HR manager, and talk turned to our retention numbers. Sometimes the overall numbers might look strong, but we would dissect them by area to identify potential opportunities for employee engagement. Once we found an opportunity in a particular territory, we would review its past employee opinion surveys. Were people listening to feedback and executing the plan?

We would also dissect the retention numbers by position and cultural demographics to see if anything stood out. In one particular meeting, our retention numbers looked very strong, but we identified a bottleneck at one of our positions. Why was this happening? Were these people getting too comfortable? Did they feel stuck? Were we not holding them accountable?

For perspective, we would normally have five to ten employees at this level, but at this time we had twenty-five. If we didn't have a pipeline of talent continuously advancing, it would slow down our ability to expand. We needed to unclog the bottleneck. After a long discussion and some insights from my regional manager, we created a game plan. We would bring in the twenty-five employees who were stuck at this crowded level, review their roles and responsibilities, and show them how they could separate themselves from the pack.

We took some time to find out where each employee was in the process, asking our peers what they'd done in the past and searching for something that would resonate with the team. We didn't want busywork; we wanted something that would enhance our people's skills and abilities. Simplicity was key because simplicity allows for speed and clarity.

Finally, we found a great video by John Maxwell on the five levels of leadership. This was perfect. Leadership skills and behaviors can be learned through a well-defined program, which is why good companies have leadership development training programs. I couldn't rely on a few great employees to execute our plans and initiatives and to make our region great. I needed everyone at every level to understand what leadership was and their roles within our team. I needed everybody rowing in the same direction. So I ran my team through Maxwell's five levels of leadership:

LEVEL 1: Positional. This is when your boss and the team follow you because of your position, so they give you the least effort possible. This type of leader is already cleaning out their desk at 4:30 p.m. At 4:45 p.m., they start saying their goodbyes. At 5:00 p.m., they're gone! You may have heard of the term "quiet quitting"—giving your all during work hours but disengaging at day's end, while others may choose to go above and beyond.

LEVEL 2: Relationship. The team connects with you, and they want to follow you. They listen, observe, and learn. You begin to grow beyond your title.

LEVEL 3: Production. You're becoming more effective because you produce, and you've gained credibility. Momentum begins to assist in solving problems.

LEVEL 4: People development. This is a five-step process:

- Step 1: I do it.
- Step 2: I do it, and you are with me.
- Step 3: You do it, and I am coaching you.
- Step 4: You do it.
- Step 5: You do it, and someone is with you.

LEVEL 5: Results. The pinnacle. You've done so well, with so many for so long, that people follow you because of who you are and what you stand for.

We made sure our employees with leadership potential were executing each of the phases until they began to have success. Constant coaching and development helped each employee perform and lead better. When that happens, individual success leads to organizational success. Tactics and strategies are understood and embraced. Everything moves in the right direction. There is harmony. Purposeful repetition creates strong habits and rituals, which build momentum. Culture grows and blossoms. Promotions happen, and new leaders take on new challenges. The business moves forward with a sense of pride.

This training was so successful that we ran all leadership levels through the exercise. That was a little of my secret sauce. If we found something that worked, we didn't leave it on an island. We spread it to all levels, from department head to branch manager.

SKILL 3: How to run meetings. I was working with a couple of other regional VPs, and we decided to hold an area manager retreat on how to run an effective meeting. Interestingly enough, according to Steven Rogelberg in *The Surprising Science of Meetings,* "only 20%

of leaders ever receive any training on how to run a meeting."[12] We knew our area managers had to be able to teach the branch managers how to run meetings because the branch manager was the one on the front line. We taught the area managers to clarify the purpose of the meeting, how to create agendas with specific time commitments, keep meetings moving, get everyone involved, and give enough notice in order for teammates to prepare effectively. We taught them to schedule the next meeting as soon as the current one was over. If you don't make important meetings recurring, some of your people will decide they don't need to attend the next one. We showed them how to recap every meeting simply and quickly, going over commitments and key takeaways in a few bullets. They loved it.

Meetings are such a universal part of business that it's always shocked me that nobody trains managers how to run a good meeting. First lesson: Spice it up. Once, to add some fun to an otherwise routine 24CC assembly, I came in dressed in a boxer's robe to "Gonna Fly Now" from *Rocky*, inspired by a huge gash on my forehead. A couple of days before, I'd been in a pickup basketball game against some of my team, and when I drove to the basket took an elbow to the face from a six-foot-five employee. I wasn't angry; stuff happens. But after I got patched up I thought, *Why not milk this?* I was so fired up that after shadowboxing around the room I almost passed out. I wasn't afraid of looking silly and could make fun of myself, and the room went nuts.

You can change the dynamics of your meetings by making them

12 Peter High, "Half Of All Meetings Are A Waste Of Time—Here's How To Improve Them," Forbes.com, November 25, 2019, accessed January 2, 2023, https://www.forbes.com/sites/peterhigh/2019/11/25/half-of-all-meetings-are-a-waste-of-timeheres-how-to-improve-them/?sh=531be43a2ea9.

timelier, quicker, and more efficient so people see meetings as substantive and useful. But you can also make your meetings valuable by using them for more than just talking about the road map and getting updates. Use meetings to:

- Get people engaged who don't always contribute. Meetings were an opportunity to call on people who I knew were bright and hardworking but might fear standing out or be uncomfortable sharing their ideas. I was always saying, "Tiffany, what are your thoughts on that?" or trying to get Paul to share a story. Without that, you end up getting contributions from the same two or three people, and everyone else sits there. The energy falls flat.
- Spot and correct disengagement: the folks who are yawning, doodling, scrolling their phones, or whispering to each other. They're either not prepared or don't care, and neither one is okay. When I cut back the number of meetings, the meetings I did have became vital. Sometimes, if I saw disengagement, I would bring you into the meeting out of the blue: "Scott, what do you think?" That's the Velvet Hammer in action. If you didn't respond, I would take you aside later and call you on it. Most of the time people got the message.
- Let people shine. I loved giving people who deserved it their moment in the sun. For instance, I had forty managers and ten area managers in my region, and at our meetings I might call on someone I knew had been delivering outstanding results to get up and give us an update, just so he or she could take a bow.
- Put people at ease. I'm a fan of self-deprecation. Nothing puts people at ease around the boss like the boss being willing to look silly. I was good at that because I had fun with it. After I was made a branch manager, I proceeded to move all over

Connecticut: Hartford, New Britain, you name it. There was a fun tradition that at the branch manager's meeting new branch managers have to sing, and I can't sing a lick. That didn't stop me. I got up there and belted out "On the Road Again" with everything I had and got the room roaring.

Bring the right energy to a meeting and praise people who bring the same energy. Also, remember that meetings are not always the answer. Everyone collaborates differently. For some people, the answer might be Slack, Zoom, or something else. After speaking with a variety of senior executives, a common theme emerged. They not only required that the purpose of a meeting be clear but there must be a purpose assigned to every agenda item: either information communication, discussion, or decision.

OFF-RAMP

Since we're talking about the mechanisms of culture, this seems like an appropriate place to talk a little more about my six-point inspection system. This system uses scores from six critical components of organizational culture—engagement; customer service; cultural values; diversity, equity, and inclusion; retention; and profit or growth—to "check under the hood" and assess changes in your culture from quarter to quarter or year to year. Is your culture becoming healthier and stronger? Or are there hidden weaknesses that could cause your company's engine to seize up and stall? The six-point inspection is a way to find out. Keep reading for more background, or if you'd like to take the system for a spin now, skip to chapter 9.

A DEEP BENCH

It's amazing what happens when you build a culture that brings people together to achieve a common goal. I remember a key point when I knew 24CC had a special culture brewing. We had won the first award in our region's history, and we were on a celebratory dinner cruise. Everyone was fired up and on the dance floor, when all of a sudden a chant went up.

At first I thought everyone was singing, but it soon became clear that everyone was chanting our region's name: "Two-Four CC! Two-Four CC!" It was one of the proudest moments of my career. To see our team spontaneously come together as a cohesive unit and demonstrate the pride of who we were together was something I will never forget. After the cruise, many of our team's emails, texts, and hashtags would end with "CC Pride!"

In a great organization, everyone is a mentor and a culture carrier. Everyone is accessible, from the CEO on down. To keep it that way, encourage your people to make training part of their lifestyle away from work. Anything we tried to teach—leadership, time management, meetings—I wanted my employees to work on at home too. It's important to make new behaviors and processes a part of who you are every minute of the day, not just who you are during the hours you're at work.

In the end, effective training leads to advancement, which means more culture carriers, deeper engagement, and better performance. When you do all this good work, you'll end up with a deep bench of leaders who are ready to take over when the need arises—and especially when the unexpected occurs. They will take your organization past obstacles and to destinations that aren't even on your map yet.

IN THE REARVIEW MIRROR

- You can train people to be culture carriers—fully engaged individuals who embody the values that underlie your culture and bring the spirit of that culture with them, even when you're not in the room.
- You can foster a training culture with OTJ training, one-on-one coaching, and morning and midmorning huddles.
- Formal mentoring programs help develop new talent, teach leadership and coaching skills to veteran employees, and share institutional knowledge.
- The think tank, a gathering of bright, ambitious individual contributors under the supervision of a leader, is a great way to increase adoption of current initiatives while brainstorming fresh new ideas.
- "Stay interviews" take the temperature of the organization by asking employees how well the company is living up to its values and keeping its commitments.
- Nobody trains on time management, how to lead, and how to run meetings, but they should.

CHAPTER 6

FOLLOW YOUR
MORAL COMPASS

*Live every part of the journey based on the values,
beliefs, and behaviors that are the foundation of your
culture.*

n April 2018, two Black men were sitting peacefully in a Phila-
delphia Starbucks. When the store manager asked them to leave
if they weren't going to buy anything, they told him they were
waiting for a colleague. The manager called the police, and the
men were arrested. The incident sparked a major PR crisis for
Starbucks, which has long portrayed itself as a caring, socially
responsible, values-driven company. Chairman Howard Schultz was
deeply distressed by the arrest, saying, "I'm embarrassed, ashamed.
I think what occurred was reprehensible at every single level. I take
it very personally, as everyone in our company does, and we're

committed to making it right."[13]

But Starbucks leadership didn't stop there, and that's where the lesson lies. On May 29, 2018, the company closed eight thousand US locations to train 175,000 employees in recognizing racial bias in themselves and others. The move cost Starbucks millions in lost revenue, and it might have saved the company's reputation.

That's following your moral compass.

The Japanese term *ikigai*, which translates as "reason for being," comes to mind. Ikigai refers to having a purpose in life that provides a sense of fulfillment and meaning, but I think that idea should apply to organizations, not just individuals. If you're leading a team or running a company, and your team or company has a larger purpose,

---

13   Gayle King, interview with Howard Schultz, *CBS This Morning*, CBS News, April 17, 2018.

driven by the moral, ethical values you and your people care about, you'll create a very special environment that produces incredible outcomes. You'll outearn the profiteers and feel great doing it. My region was fortunate enough to be one of the most profitable regions in the country, but I used to tell my team that profit didn't matter if our customer experience—customer service score—and employee experience—employee retention and engagement score—weren't great, because that meant we were doing it the wrong way.

As you and your team of culture carriers unfold your road map and set out toward your goals, your morals and values are what guides them. They're your compass, keeping you on course and reminding you who you are.

YOU'RE ALWAYS ON STAGE

From the time I joined Enterprise, the company's eight founding values were drilled into us. I've mentioned them before, but they're worth mentioning again:

1. Our brands are the most valuable things we own.

2. We work hard and reward hard work.

3. Customer service is our way of life.

4. Great things happen when we listen to our customers and each other.

5. Personal honesty and integrity are the foundation of our success.

6. We strengthen our communities—one neighborhood at a time.

7. Our company is a fun and friendly place, where teamwork rules.

8. Our doors are open.

Undoubtedly, your organization has core values of its own. What makes those values so important is that if they are authentic, and you adhere to them, they will keep you on the straight and narrow path when you're in the public eye. That's critical because in a community in which an employer has any visibility you're on stage even when you are not at work. Even as a parent at your child's competition or a customer at Starbucks, your behavior reflects on your organization. You're always in the public eye. Someone is always watching you act or react. When you internalize your organization's moral values and do your best to live them every day, it's easier to do the right thing, be a good role model, and show people the way.

I was always aware that to many of my people I was a moral leader, so I was careful to live our values as well as I could. I was friendly and cordial with everyone, but I wouldn't gossip, because the wrong words can embarrass not only individuals but an entire organization. Our values became the filter through which I made nearly all my professional decisions—and many of my personal decisions. They were also a guiding star for my team and my region. Whatever your organization's values are, never compromise on them. Never take a shortcut.

According to Scott Kirkpatrick, CEO of BrainPop, which is a very successful online educational tool that makes learning experiences accessible to students, he mentions values have another dimension: *antivalues*. An antivalue is the commonsense limiter to how far your organization should take a value before applying the brakes. "Any value can be taken to an extreme, and then it is not effective," said Scott in our interview. "An antivalue just puts a boundary on how far a value can go. For example, empathy can go too far without accountability—truly balancing your head with your heart. So a good antivalue for empathy would be accountability."

MAKING THE SOUP

Values tell you what your organization stands for, whether that's diversity, innovation, humility, teamwork, or what have you. They represent each employee, from the CEO to your newest hire. They're your way-finding system. Every so often, you have to pull the car into a turnout or a rest stop, check your compass, and make sure you're still headed in the right direction. I would base my performance on my company's founding values because I wanted to ensure I was really living each one. I owed it to the company and my team to follow and enforce these values, not just have them listed on a poster in the lobby.

Claude Silver of VaynerMedia shared this analogy with me. She talked about culture like she was making a big pot of homemade minestrone soup: "What I would put into the minestrone soup of my culture is self-awareness, patience, humility, gratitude, kindness, empathy, compassion, sincerity, accountability, patience, forgiveness, and as much as we can, limit our ego or our need to boast and to be prideful," she said in our interview. "Humility is a big piece of that. When you make soup, if you don't put in the bay leaf—I don't know what a bay leaf does, but it's not right without it—there's something you miss. For me, that's humility. That's the base."

I love that image of culture as soup. The final product might be a little different for every chef, but the cooking instructions are the same. Never compromise on the quality of your ingredients, be attentive to nuance—a dash more of this, a pinch less of that—have patience, and trust the process. If you can, add your own "bay leaf"—your individual, unique touch—to what you're building. I tried to do that with everything from how I ran meetings to initiatives like the think tank. Living and working by the values you hold most dear is how you enjoy sustainable success. So let's get cooking.

(Author's note: While I've based this chapter around the eight values that guided my team, I've made the values more generic from here on because I want them to be useful for all organizations. On we go.)

1. BRAND IS THE MOST IMPORTANT THING YOU HAVE

If my team took a trip to Florida, whether it was fun or on business, we weren't just representing ourselves. It was like we were always wearing a badge that said "24CC New York." Everything we did reflected on our brand.

That mattered even more early on because when I came on board our region had a less-than-stellar brand. People had lost their belief in initiatives and promotional opportunities. Cynicism kills trust and loyalty, and cynicism was a plague in the southern New England region. We had to rebrand ourselves, but guess what? You can't change your brand with words. Talk is cheap. The only way to change your brand is with consistent action based on genuine values—that, and time.

So I started with my personal brand. Everything I did was analyzed. My actions would set the tone and send a powerful message about what our new brand would be going forward. Would I follow through with my commitments? Would I adhere to our founding values? Or would I compromise and do what was easy? Could we truly be one of the best regions in the country? From the beginning, I was under pressure to show everyone in my region what we were going to be about from that day forward.

"Our brands are the most valuable thing we own" became my favorite founding value. A brand is a promise of what you can expect each time you interact with a person, product, or company. Every decision you make sends a powerful message and represents three essential traits about you:

1. Who you are.

2. What you're known for.

3. What you stand for.

If your brand is what people say about you when you're not in the room, culture equals the behaviors that happen when leaders aren't around to enforce the organization's behavioral codes. But because you're in a leadership role, your personal brand

and the company's brand are intertwined. There is a powerful correlation between personal branding and culture. To the people you lead and the customers who come into contact with you, you *are* the company. That's why you should never overlook the power of branding or discount the fragility of a brand.

Think about Elon Musk. Portrayed by many as a visionary in energy and car engineering, with his name synonymous with the Tesla brand, Musk has shaken this perception with his lack of a filter on social media, which often lands him in hot water with the public. As a leader, be mindful of how your behaviors represent your company values and the ripple effect they can have on your team. You will never please everyone, but too many controversial comments can affect your company. Musk's case is an illustration of the tightrope you have to walk with your personal brand, and why the only way to make a brand last is to build it on your authentic personal values and ethics, which you must also live and embody.

WHO CONTROLS YOUR BRAND?

If a brand is a promise, what happens when you break a promise? People who believed in you feel betrayed and humiliated. You can make ten thousand great decisions and ten thousand great impressions, but all it takes is one action or decision that contradicts your brand to damage it, perhaps irreparably. Once you establish a brand, you have to spend the rest of your career continuing to reinforce it through your words, actions, values, and choices.

We see this everywhere. Think of strong personal brands—Derek Jeter, Oprah Winfrey, Taylor Swift, Jay-Z, Warren Buffett. They don't just represent themselves but their organizations. To many, Jeter *is* the New York Yankees. I love Jay-Z's quote: "I am not a businessman; I am a business, man." He gets it. He *is* the business. So are you. When you hear the names of those icons, a set of values and traits come to mind, right? You may be no Warren Buffett, but the same is true for you.

When people hear about you, they think of certain qualities. Which ones? Those qualities are your brand. As a leader and an example for the employees you lead, you have to take control of your brand—establish it clearly, grow it, and protect it. The thing about a personal brand is that you already have one, whether you realize it or not.

OFF-RAMP

How many times have you read a post on LinkedIn, a tweet on Twitter, saw a picture on Instagram or Facebook, or viewed a video on TikTok and knew a close friend, colleague, or family member just crossed a line? And in the process jeopardized their own personal or business brand? Companies need to train their employees on having social media etiquette that balances who you are without compromising you or your company's values and reputation. This must be part of the onboarding process and employee road map. Do you need to pump the brakes? Is everyone on the right highway? Think about it.

KEEP IT REAL

The tightrope analogy is apt because you really do have to walk a fine line with your brand. There are so many ways to contradict it and give rise to doubt and suspicion that the only smart play is to build it around principles and values that truly represent who you are—to walk your talk. Here's one example: A counterpart received a promotion I had badly wanted. It was one of the toughest days of my career. To top it off, after I received the news I had not been selected, I had back-to-back meetings with my department heads, all of whom knew I was up for the promotion. So, while I wanted to take the rest of the day off and nurse my wounded ego, I had constantly talked about humility and putting team before individual ambition, so it was important for my team to see how I responded. My leadership was center stage, and it was up to me to practice what I preached.

I could've canceled those meetings. My team would have let it slide. But I didn't do that. I never even considered it. I had a responsibility to live the values I was espousing. I had to be a living example of how to keep it professional when deeply disappointed. The following day I had a conference call with my leadership team and informed them I hadn't received the promotion. I said the person who had received the promotion was talented and would do a great job. This was not easy, but that made my attitude even more important. I knew I'd made the right decision when my team ended the call by saying, "Stone, we won't let you lose the next one."

Or, to use an apocryphal, abridged quote from Ralph Waldo Emerson, "What you do speaks so loudly, I can't hear what you're saying."

Ingredient check—personal brand:

- one part humility
- three parts consistency
- four parts authenticity
- pinch of self-awareness

2. HONOR AND INTEGRITY

Honesty and integrity aren't just about internal decisions. They're about how your company deals with customers and the world. Do you follow the rules? Do you act with honor and decency? Are you trustworthy? Any company that wants to sustain its business over the long term has to act with integrity. Big corporations or unethical banks might get away with breaking the rules for a while, but eventually everybody gets caught, and everything falls apart. Remember: In 2008 Lehman Brothers, a multibillion-dollar investment bank in business since 1847, went bankrupt when it used false accounting practices to create a stronger financial position. No one thought such financial leaders could fall, but they did.

TRUST: HARD TO EARN, EASY TO LOSE

Honesty and integrity keep you on the straight path when you're tempted to take shortcuts. There are no shortcuts. Honesty and integrity keep you from killing your business through malfeasance, by associating with bad people, by being sued, or by ruining your reputation through scandal. They foster trust, the most important aspect of your brand. Your customers trust you with their money, their time, and perhaps their homes, health, finances, freedom, even their lives. Acting with honesty and integrity is how you earn and keep that trust.

That's why being inconsistent with your values kills culture—it kills trust. There must be consequences when ethics are compromised. In managing thousands of employees, my team had a well-defined approach when handling such situations. It started with an investigation. First, we would talk to the employee and let them tell their side of the story. Then we would talk to others who might have seen what happened. Once we had all the information, we would make our decision, and if you had crossed an ethical line, no matter who you were, you were terminated. While losing a good employee is always disappointing, allowing ethical violations is unacceptable.

Consider Pete Rose. What comes to mind when you read that name? If you're a baseball fan, I'll bet it's not his Hall of Fame–worthy career hit total. It's that he disgraced himself by betting on baseball. Major League Baseball (MLB) did a nice job looking into the investigation, and by banning Rose for life they sent a clear message that his behavior would not be tolerated. What would've happened if the MLB had turned a blind eye? Fan trust in the game would have taken a potentially fatal hit.

Every quarter we had a business ethics meeting with my controller and HR manager. We did a deep dive into any sticky ethical situations that had occurred over the previous quarter, looking for trends and making sure we were consistent with the outcomes. Our training classes had modules on ethical violations and the right behaviors to prevent them. We had a confidential online system that would allow team members to disclose potential ethical violations without fear of reprisal. We made the rules clear, the consequences clear, and our values clear.

There will always be people who think the rules don't apply to them. Make sure the rules are clear and fair, and then apply them to everyone. Honor and integrity define who you are as an organization. They are not luxuries.

Ingredient check—honor and integrity:

- one part rules
- two parts oversight
- three parts fairness
- four parts accountability

3. GRATITUDE FOR THE CUSTOMER

I've mentioned the **Johnny the Bagger Award,** but the idea behind it bears repeating. In 24CC, our philosophy was that when the customer came into one of our stores they were our guests, and we were their host. We always wanted to be grateful for the customer's business because we were not entitled to it. If we acted like we were entitled to it, we deserved to lose it. The car rental industry is a commodity industry. Anyone can rent you a car. We were out to create a memorable experience so you would come back, and to do that we had to make customer service the center of everything we did.

Being grateful for the customer or client becomes especially important when things go wrong. It's easy to be cheerful when everything's going right, but when something went wrong that was when we really put our personal signature on the interaction. When there's a problem, that tells your customer, clear as day, whether you truly care about them or not. Have you ever bought something from a store where they were very eager to help you, until they had your money? Everyone has. As soon as there's a problem, you can't get anyone on the phone. But great teams and organizations show their commitment by being even more enthusiastic about helping customers when they're unhappy.

Any opportunities to prove your commitment to your customer should be "wow" moments. In fact, the way we went over the top to fix problems changed me as a customer. When I would patronize another business, I would pay close attention to their customer service procedures, positive and negative, and formulate a critique. Think of it as a "Siskel and Ebert" for customer service. Sometimes I felt compelled to share my thoughts with leadership; other times I wondered, "How does this company survive?"

People can be rude, angry, and difficult, and you have to keep smiling through it all. The customer isn't always right, but they must feel like they're always right, and that's what matters. The point is, customer service is hard work, and it's good practice to reward the people who do it well. We collected a great deal of data from customer service surveys, and we would send out monthly customer service reports.

We also held a summer customer service contest every year during our summer peak season, and if your team scored at a certain level we would reward the entire team at a sports or cultural event, food and beverages included. We'd also reward the top branch in customer service by inviting the entire staff to my home for the bimonthly awards dinners I mentioned earlier.

Our service mentality even trickled down to my youngest son, Carson, who was always around during these dinners. During one bimonthly awards dinner, it was pouring rain, and as people were getting out of their cars my son sprinted out with an umbrella and escorted them into the house. Interestingly enough, he also decided to collect tips—that was, until I found out and made him give back the money. Can't blame a kid for trying.

You have to walk your talk on putting the customer first. In my region, everything was about the customer, from how we dressed to how we cleaned our cars. If you were our customer, you knew you would have a certain kind of experience, and we were proud to be held to a high standard.

Ingredient check—customer gratitude:

- two parts training
- two parts memorable experience
- three parts attention to detail
- one part recognition
- pinch of little gestures

4. THE COMPANY IS FUN, FRIENDLY, AND TEAMWORK WINS THE DAY

A couple of years ago, after my son Ryan graduated from college, we went to a local restaurant, Coast Guard House in Narragansett, Rhode Island, for lunch to celebrate. It was a nice day, and the patio had a great view, so I asked our server if we could be seated outside. If you've asked to be reseated at some places, you know they act like you're asking them to move mountains. Not at this restaurant. We ended up at an outside table on the condition that we needed to be done by two o'clock. No problem.

We had a terrific time. The food was great, the waitress gave great recommendations, and the weather was gorgeous. But what I really noticed was the employees high-fiving each other as they walked past. I loved that positive energy.

Have you seen that *Fortune* magazine annual list of best companies to work for? If you have, you might have noticed the same companies keep coming up. There seem to be certain common elements with the employers that appear on these lists year after year.

They have exceptional cultures powered by energetic, passionate employees. They encourage and reward employee development and mentorship. They train and compensate their people well, and they treat them with respect. When you go into the retail locations of those companies, or interact with their customer service departments, their people usually seem happy to be there and happy to help you. Their sense of enjoyment is contagious.

In our region, we wanted a competitive environment in which everyone was happy to pitch in. If I walked into a store, and it was twenty customers deep, even as a regional VP I would go and greet customers and assist in handling the rush. That's what was needed. When other employees see that, they're falling all over themselves to do the same. That's teamwork. That's caring about each other.

When a team survives hard times, it breeds camaraderie. You bond. After we had a crazy day, we might go out together for a drink, or I might just recognize their efforts and say, "Hey, guys, great job today!" We worked hard, and we got to have fun as a reward. Blend in some fun team contests to build on your chemistry, reward the team for achieving certain milestones, and let your leaders do the rest.

FUN MATTERS

I've always been a strong believer in healthy competition and rewarding people for doing great work, as long as the rewards don't come so easily that they're like participation trophies.

In 24CC, we knew we were going to work hard, and we told our people that from the beginning, so we wanted to establish a policy that it was okay to have some fun while we were trying to be the best region in the country. Fun doesn't always happen at work—it's called *work* for a reason—but when you're working with colleagues who truly care about your success, want you to do well, and try to make your job easier, work *becomes* fun. People do their jobs better because they feel valued and cared about. That's just as important as holding team events, happy hours, and volleyball tournaments, which we did consistently.

I've said that you have to be grateful for your customers, but as an employer or leader you also have to be grateful for your employees. They're working for a paycheck, but they don't want to be treated like that's the only thing they're working for. Most really want to like their jobs and coworkers. When I was a branch manager, we might all be working hard at 6:00 p.m., but instead of everybody rushing to go home, a Wiffle ball game would break out in the store. That was our mentality: work hard and earn the right to have fun. That led to great camaraderie.

If you want people to treat their job as more than a transaction, fun matters. It's not an "extra." If you want people to work harder than they ever have before, make them feel like they're part of something. Give them chances to become a tribe in which people have each other's backs. We would have our team dress up in Halloween costumes and reward the best dressed team. We'd have ugly sweater days or days when they would wear the gear of their alma mater.

One of our best teamwork examples came after a blizzard that buried all our cars in close to forty inches of snow. The next day our entire administrative staff helped dig our fleet out of huge snowdrifts. It was our version of Boston's Big Dig. The activity broke up the routine and gave us all one more chance to work together and exchange a high five at the end.

I was always ready to poke fun at myself too. Being color blind, my wife would lay out my clothes every night, right down to my socks tucked into my shoes. It was the only way I could be sure that everything I was wearing matched.

Well, every summer my wife spends some time with her family in Old Lyme, a beautiful town on the Connecticut coast, and when she was gone I had to wing it with my clothes. One morning I mixed up my jacket and pants, and I went in to lead this training class with no idea that I looked like I'd gotten dressed in the dark. I was at the front of the room, and everyone in the audience was smiling. I had no idea why; I thought I was doing great. Then I took a break, walked back to my office, and my assistant, barely suppressing a smile, said, "Eric, you don't match."

Wait, what? She described what I was wearing, and when I went back to the room, I said, "How are you guys not telling me that I look ridiculous?" The whole room broke up. They were loving it, and frankly so was I.

Ingredient check—fun and teamwork:

- one part creativity
- two parts hard work
- three parts chemistry
- three parts team spirit

5. WORK HARD AND REWARD HARD WORK

I didn't miss a day of work due to illness in more than twenty-five years. It's true. I worked through compression fractures in my back, broken fingers, sprained ankles, and sometimes feeling like I got run over by a bus. I guess, like the late Kobe Bryant, I tried to cultivate the "mamba mentality."

But my version of hard work for my employees wasn't "work until you drop." It was "whatever hours you're on the job, I want your A-game." Our locations were always busy, with customers coming in and out constantly. There was never downtime. If traffic slowed, we would shift into an administrative or training role. Leave it all on the court and maximize every moment of the day. No regrets!

Despite the intensity, our retention rates were usually in the 80 percent range and in the top 10 percent of the company. I think some of that was due to our style, which was built around a "find a solution" mindset, commitment, coachability, self-challenge, and meeting your own high expectations. I would empower my team to make decisions and then hold them accountable for how those decisions played out. I would encourage them to excel, to get out of their comfort zone, to surpass what they did yesterday. Most people really want to be their best and have pride in what they do.

In getting my people to work hard while still maintaining high morale and a great sense of teamwork, I adopted the five factors of engagement and positioned them to play an important role. So, when my team achieved a goal, we didn't just move on. We tried to celebrate, whether that was an office lunch, a gift, or an event. A manager might drop off some munchies at the counter because they knew the team had been running and gunning all day. That was what those dinners at my house were about: not just saying thank you but recognizing that my people had really put in the effort to get results.

Ingredient check—work hard and reward hard work:

- two parts preparation
- two parts attitude

- two parts boss example
- two parts balance
- two parts recognition

6. LISTEN TO EACH OTHER

How can you get better if you don't ask for feedback? There will be a time to pivot, adjust, and reevaluate your strategy, and who better to ask for guidance than your employees and customers? If you choose not to do this, you'll be making assumptions, and as Don Miguel Ruiz wrote in *The Four Agreements*: "Don't make assumptions. Find the courage to ask questions and to express what you really want. Communicate with others as clearly as you can to avoid misunderstandings, sadness and drama."[14] Assumptions will only lead you to mediocrity, isolation, and a culture of insecurity.

Beware of being too arrogant to ask your employees for help or to accept their feedback. Instead, invite their feedback, as long as it's delivered constructively, privately, and respectfully. After every training class, I would *always* ask, "What can we do better?" I always carried a little pad on which I would write all my to-do items, and if you made my list I *would* follow up on what you said. I might even send you a thank-you email for bringing up the issue.

Your team must trust that you will do something with their feedback. Even incremental improvements matter. Everyone did this: branch managers gave feedback to area managers, area managers gave feedback to the regional managers, regional managers gave feedback to department heads, and all levels gave feedback to me.

---

14   Don Miguel Ruiz, *The Four Agreements: A Practical Guide to Personal Freedom* (Carlsbad, CA: Hay House, 1997).

Remember my think tank? Before our meetings, think tank members would each ask a group of employees for feedback on important topics so I could get an idea of the pulse of our region. I also encouraged my department heads to spend time in the field talking to our employees about our initiatives and the employee experience. We would conduct quarterly engagement surveys to measure engagement and annual employee opinion surveys. The more I knew the better manager, leader, and colleague I could be.

Making communication safe and easy can be critical. Remember the 737 Max 8 crisis in March 2019, when two airliners with the Boeing control system inexplicably crashed? It turned out that some Boeing engineers had been concerned that the system might seize control of a plane from pilots in midair, but the company's culture discouraged talking about potential problems, so they didn't speak up. The result was tragedy.

Pay attention to subtle communication, and not just with customers. Early in my career, I had an expensive Montblanc pen that my father had given me and was using it to write up a customer's rental. Something set him off, and he grabbed my pen, threw it on the floor, and stepped on it! I was so stunned I didn't know what to do, and only later, when my manager saw how upset I was and asked me what was wrong, did I tell him what had happened. I really appreciated that he noticed, and I've never forgotten it.

Also, accept that you can be wrong and that negative feedback can be the greatest blessing of all. You should want to hear what you're doing wrong or how you're not living up to expectations. That makes you better. Tracy Maylett, cofounder of DecisionWise, a Utah-based consulting firm specializing in employee engagement, sees policies like these as the key to creating strong engagement because everything starts with culture. "There are three terms that we interchange mistakenly: culture, employee experience, and employee engagement," he said in our interview. "Culture is everything that our values tell us and show us about the way we do things. A good culture impacts the employee experience. My experience as an employee is related to how things are done around here. When the employee experience matches what is right for me, engagement is the result."

Ingredient check—listen to customers and each other:

- one part surveys
- two parts asking questions
- two parts unspoken cues
- three parts getting into the field
- a dash of incremental improvement

7. STRENGTHEN THE COMMUNITY

Every organization's values should be an active part of the community in which it does business. Our region did this tenfold, running a robust workplace campaign with the United Way. We were fortunate to have one of the more successful United Way campaigns of any region in the country. Our leadership team was constantly talking about why it's important to support the communities that we live and work in and give back to those who are in need. It's not just about the bottom line. It's about taking care of the people who, by being our customers, take care of us.

Community giving is a vital dimension of culture. While our competitors might be meeting with an account to check in, we would be balancing the business relationship with the account while also trying to see how we could partner with them on issues we were both passionate about within the communities we served. This could range from joining them on a breast cancer walk, volunteering together to collect backpacks for kids in need, or supporting an effort to raise money for veterans. That's how you take things to another level. Today giving and making a difference are necessary parts of the corporate mission. They're no longer optional.

In the new hire interview process, I was often asked—especially by millennials—"What do you do to support the local community?" This was where our relationship with the United Way was a powerful recruiting tool. Our efforts got us recognized at the yearly Live United events on several occasions, with things like the Give Award and the Corporate Social Responsibility Award. I was also fortunate enough to serve on the United Way board of directors for more than a decade and was asked on a few occasions to lead their annual corporate campaign.

Having a strong philanthropic platform and a spirit of giving and being part of the community are tactile examples of living your values and a wonderful way to create an engaged workforce. By being involved, you increase trust, belief, values, behaviors, authenticity, ownership, and empowerment.

THE OPPOSITE OF CYNICISM

If cynicism is deadly to culture, then community outreach is food for culture. It's the opposite of cynicism. Being involved shows your people and your community you are who you say you are. It fosters hope that business can be a force for good.

Giving also feels great. So have fun with it! We once raised a large amount of money for the United Way, and they wanted to recognize our region at the yearly Live United banquet. United Way took pictures of the person representing each organization and made these really nice posters—a little bigger than actual size. They hung them all around the event space. A few team members went along for the ride to enjoy the ceremony, and they ended up taking the poster of me back to our administrative building.

Periodically, my HR manager made visits to other areas to explain our region's involvement with the United Way. Since I wasn't able to attend all those meetings, she thought it would be cute to bring the oversized poster of me and unveil it at each event. It was fun—my way of being omnipresent. These were late-night events so people were relaxed, and they would end up standing next to this life-size poster of me like they were standing next to a cutout of Arnold Schwarzenegger. They would give a thumbs-up or a wave and take a picture. My HR manager would text it to me with a message like, "Eric, enjoy your dinner!" I got that every time there was a United Way event. It was a really thoughtful way of saying, "Eric, we're thinking of you." That's one more example of this special environment, where people were excited to rally around a goofy picture of me.

This was terrific for our brand. Due to our very successful campaign, along Interstate 95 stood one of our crowning achievements: a billboard that read "Welcome to the Chairman's Circle," telling everyone who saw it about 24CC's commitment to giving back to the community.

Your team and your organization are not separate from the community. You're part of it, dependent on it. *Be* an integral part of it.

Ingredient check—strengthen the community:

- two parts giving
- three parts helping
- two parts feeling great
- one part self-promotion
- stir briskly

8. OPEN DOORS

Finally, communication; diversity, equity, and inclusivity; and learning what makes your employees tick are indisputable assets. Your organization should be a two-way street. In our region, it didn't matter what your position or background was. Whether you were a customer, employee, or business partner, we valued everyone and their differences and wanted open, continuous dialogue about how we could make things better for everybody.

In fact, we created a Minority Interactive Network and Women's Interactive Network to promote greater opportunities for groups of people who were often overlooked in other organizations. While our minority and female employees weren't necessarily having a problem joining the team, we noticed they were falling short in terms of being promoted to area manager and beyond. We decided to create MIN and WIN, bodies that met quarterly, to discuss challenges they faced, with a mission to attract, retain, and advance a diverse workforce.

This eventually grew into a coaching and development program for growing a diverse class of future leaders. We would coach and mentor on topics like the importance of networking, interviewing to win, time management, resilience and grit, SWOT (strength, weakness, opportunity, and threat) analysis, and career mapping. We also conducted "generation training" to help managers learn to understand each generation's perspective and priorities, particularly millennial employees.

Having open doors means you have to change with the times because the times change whether you do or not. Our doors were always open to everyone, no matter their race, gender, ethnicity, or sexual orientation. We wanted to understand what was going on with our people. We wanted to be as supportive as we could be. If someone came into my office unannounced, I would find a way to hear what they had to say. I literally worked with my door open as much as possible.

Ingredient check—open doors:

- four parts communication
- three parts opening your door
- two parts diversity and equity

THE POWER OF SMALL THINGS

This isn't about the bottom line, not directly. It's about trust, faith, integrity, belief, and inspiration. It's about being the kind of organization people will walk through fire to be part of and make better. As Claude Silver told me during our chat, if you make people feel good, they will do good things for you.

"What does it feel like when someone stops you for a second in the hallway and says, 'Hey, Eric, how was your weekend?' You feel like that person cares about you. It feels good," she said in our interview. "It increases serotonin, the same thing we get from chocolate. It increases oxytocin, like we get from hugging a baby. Taking time, giving attention, makes people feel really good."

It's true. I was once at a meeting of our leadership team in the New York region, and when it came time for dessert the attendees decided for some arbitrary reason it was my birthday. It wasn't, but I can't say no to dessert, so suddenly we had a cake and about twenty-five people singing "Happy Birthday" to me.

That just happened to be the same day that one of our senior executives decided to pay a visit to the New York region, and she loved it. She loved the spirit and the self-deprecating way I had fun with it. Fast-forward a few years later, and I was interviewing for a new opportunity in Wisconsin. It was down to the final four candidates, and the night before the interviews the senior VP who would head up the interviews took the four of us out to dinner. Little did I know, she had told this senior VP all about the birthday-cake incident. So, in the middle of dinner, out comes a little birthday cake, and everyone starts singing "Happy Birthday" to me. How can you not love that kind of company spirit?

The impact of little things, of being seen, of your boss remembering a birthday or that your parent is ill—it all plays a part in a culture that's about living your values every moment of every day. Make those who you are, consistently and authentically, and your people will see that. They will reward you richly for it. These small but sensitive strategies are quick and manageable jumpstarts that can instantly lift morale and be an unexpected boost that goes miles.

IN THE REARVIEW MIRROR

- Be aware of the differences between listing your values and actually living your values.
- Each company value should have a list of behaviors to support your actions.

- Create antivalues—the boundary of how far a value can go.
- Ensure that there are touchpoints along an employee's career journey to review, discuss, evaluate, and reward those living your values.

CHAPTER 7

ADAPT, CHANGE COURSE, AND KEEP DRIVING

You've reached your destination, but it's not what you expected. Adjust, be resilient, and be flexible when things don't work out like you planned.

t was 2008, the depths of the Great Recession. It was a bad time. I attended a yearly officers' meeting, and it was the most somber one I had ever attended. You go to these meetings, and they're usually about firing you up—breakouts, maybe even a motivational speaker, and lots of energy. But this time things were deadly serious. People were scared. The economy was collapsing, and we didn't know if we were going to have jobs. It was clear to me that my region would have to make some major changes that we had never made before in order to stay afloat.

For example, sales had declined in a way that I had not seen since I took over the region. It would have been easy to make excuses and complain about the downturn, but I'm not wired that way, and I didn't want my team relying on excuses either. We needed to get in front of the issue before we started to lose momentum. Nobody was going to feel sorry for us, because they were all facing the same challenges we were.

We knew we were missing something, so we needed to adapt and change course. My regional manager went into the field to talk to the team while I held some one-on-one meetings and spent time with my think tank. Eventually, we found a common thread. It turned out that employees were having a difficult time dealing with a few problematic types of customers. We had done solid training on overcoming objections and handling emotional customers, but my team was having problems with the bold, assertive folks, the ones who felt they were the most important people in the room and didn't have time to dillydally.

Now that we had information, it was time to write up strategies and set fresh goals. Keep in mind we weren't planning to make a change for the sake of change. That's rarely a good idea because change without a purpose is a burden for those stuck executing it. Instead, we had a clear goal: identify the personality types we were having trouble with and hone our skills in managing those personalities. After some more conversations, we settled on four personas:

1. The chatterbox. This is the customer who comes in and wants to chat with everybody. They're charming and funny, and you don't want to shut them down, but if you don't they'll slow rentals to a crawl.

2. The diplomat. This person agrees with everything you suggest, which isn't as useful as it seems. Because you won't get useful feedback or pushback from them, employees might

make mistakes that you don't even catch until the customer's out the door.

3. The calculator. This person is all about the facts and figures—why one car costs this much per day, whether it makes more sense to buy a tank of fuel in advance or fill the tank before returning the car, and so on. They can take forever to decide and drive you crazy with "if-then" scenarios.

4. The executive. They were the biggest challenge. These bold, aggressive folks are all business. Their time is important, and you know that because during the transaction they're staring at their watch. They just want to get the car and leave. We really struggled with that one because they were immune to our customer service charms. They made up maybe 20 percent of the people who walked through the doors, but they hurt our sales because no matter what we suggested for extras and upgrades they said no, and we'd fold like a lawn chair.

The solution was to improve, and we did that by developing training modules to better deal with these four personality types. This was intriguing, a new goal, and people were excited about the chance to learn something new and get past these customer frustrations.

My regional manager formulated a few word paths that could guide employees to better build a connection, identify obstacles, and provide solutions in order to assist the customer in making a buying decision. Then we downloaded the information to the team. We scheduled meetings well in advance, and since the team already knew why we were there—sales were down—we got down to practice. We broke each process into steps and then went through the entire process in role play. I'm a big fan of role play because it helps people visualize a real-life scenario right in front of them.

This was "practice with a purpose." Bill Walsh, former head coach of the NFL's San Francisco 49ers, developed the West Coast offense that transformed the NFL and helped make Joe Montana and Steve Young superstars. His way was all about focused repetitions that helped players develop high-level skills they could use under pressure. We did the same thing. We set high goals and clear expectations, and then recapped everything in an email so nothing was lost in translation.

But that wasn't all. We had a follow-up conference call about a week later to share our successes with the training. Next, we added the new material to our training classes so everyone from new hires to assistant managers would train on it. We made sure everyone knew about it because training doesn't work if you keep it a secret.

We introduced the four personality types and the training into everyone's thirty minutes of fame sessions—those deep-dive meetings our managers would have with individual employees that were just for them. We introduced the material into everyone's mentor meetings as well, and we would talk through the key points, the results we had seen to date, and how we might modify what we were doing to clear away any obstacles keeping our people from being successful. Finally, my regional managers, area managers, and I got into the field and observed the training in action. Had it been communicated to everyone? Was it being executed correctly? Were people aware of the new goals and expectations? To our satisfaction, employees in the field had not only taken to the new training but it was starting to show significant revenue results.

The program grew teeth. People started sharing stories. At our morning huddles, we started brainstorming about handling different customer types. Over time, that process became an inherent part of what we did, and it transformed our culture. The 2008 decline wasn't just an opportunity to find weaknesses in our sales but a chance to help managers and frontline employees learn, develop their awareness, and get better, and it came about because we adapted and changed course.

STUFF HAPPENS

No matter how hard your team works, no matter how clear your road map is, no matter how well you train on reaching your goals, things won't always work out as planned. You will hit adversity on your journey. Designs will be rejected. Mergers will fall through. Customers will complain. People will quit. It happens. When it does, your culture should give you the power to adapt, reload, and keep going to the next destination.

What we've talked about so far naturally leads us to this point. In developing the culture of my team and my region, the default was to focus on solutions. While you can't control the event, you can control your response. By listening, observing, learning, and keeping your finger on the pulse of your culture, you'll not only know when things start to go south but you'll also have a clear idea how your people will react to a crisis. As you continue to make sound leadership decisions, your team's belief and trust in your competence will grow, making the pivot to a new objective easier and less disruptive.

Your approach might be different from mine, but that doesn't matter as long as you keep this in mind:

Do not plan around things always going well or as anticipated.

The old adage "Expect the best, prepare for the worst" applies here. Draw your road map, set big goals, and look forward to success. But at the same time, accept that things won't always go as planned. That doesn't make you a pessimist; it makes you a good leader who lives in the real world. What kinds of unexpected problems are we talking about? It literally could be anything, but here are some examples:

- a major equipment failure
- a product recall
- an internal scandal
- an unintentionally offensive marketing campaign
- internal conflict within your company that derails a project
- failing to hit your target numbers and goals
- a customer service fiasco

A RESILIENT CULTURE

Resilience is a critical but underappreciated element of a strong culture. A resilient culture is one that can withstand setbacks and unexpected failures and bounce back while still adhering to the values that define the organization.

That type of culture starts with leadership. Maybe the greatest example of that in action is what happened in 1970, when Apollo 13 suffered its infamous explosion on the way to the moon. Suddenly the people of NASA Mission Control—who thought they had prepared for everything with tests, training, checks, rechecks, and redundancies—were thrown for a loop. In seconds, they went from a routine mission to an unprecedented emergency that put the lives of astronauts Jim Lovell, Fred Haise, and Jack Swigert in immediate jeopardy, all while the entire world was watching.

If you read the books and interviews about what happened from April 11–17, 1970, you see that all the classic stages of dealing with a crisis played out. At first the controllers in Houston were in disbelief. The machine couldn't have suffered all those simultaneous failures; the instruments reporting the data had to be wrong! But as time went by, and flight director Gene Kranz calmed the room down, and as the Apollo 13 crew reported in, everyone came to realize there had indeed been a catastrophic explosion that was draining the spacecraft's power and oxygen. They had to adjust and adapt. Their previous mission was gone. They had a new one: get the three men home alive. And they succeeded.

I'm not comparing my sales decline with three astronauts in mortal danger, but I had to deal with that situation and leave my team stronger than it was before. My role was to prepare my people mentally to execute, brainstorm, and push initiatives forward. I wanted to help them grow into confident professionals who would become *more* focused when something went wrong. Who could home in on the real problem and not panic? Who could lead when things were not going well? Anyone can lead when everything is sunshine and roses.

It's amazing how you can turn a challenge or crisis into an opportunity with the right cultural framework. By approaching opportunities and challenges in the same way, we did exactly that.

LEADING THROUGH THE UNEXPECTED

An organization might go for years without experiencing a serious crisis. Because the nature of a crisis is to come out of nowhere, however, you will be very glad you have a strong, confident culture in place when the inevitable does happen.

That's what I learned in the spring of 2020, when the most serious crisis in a century hit the world in the form of a coronavirus called COVID-19. By January 30, the World Health Organization (WHO) had declared a global health emergency. By February 6, the US had logged its first death from COVID-19, and on March 11 WHO declared it a pandemic.

You know the rest. For much of the year, the country basically shut down. The pandemic changed everything. Businesses were forced to shut down in order to stop the spread of the virus. Bars, restaurants, gyms, faith organizations, schools, and more closed. Stock markets plummeted. Nonprofits and arts organizations struggled to survive. The travel industry was gutted. Companies were forced to lay off employees in order to try to survive. Organizations that hoped to survive depended on strong leadership and a resilient culture.

How do you navigate something like COVID-19? By definition, you can't create a playbook for the unexpected, but you can put a foundational process in place. Having a process in place helps you to get past fear and anxiety and to focus so you can lead your team. For example, look at how well some companies adapted to the changes made necessary by the pandemic. Not only did countless restaurants pivot to take-out service to stay afloat but even some theater companies, unable to host live audiences, kept their doors open by selling tickets for live performances streamed online.

Commercial airlines converted their passenger flights into cargo flights hauling personal protective equipment. Grocery stores became fulfillment centers. Gyms offered online workouts for people trying to stay fit during lockdowns. Everyone showed an extraordinary ability to adapt. Your people will take their cues from you on how adaptable and resilient they can be.

Consider what happened after another unprecedented crisis, the September 11 terrorist attacks. You may remember that in the aftermath there was a great deal of fear of powder laced with deadly anthrax bacteria being sent in envelopes through the mail. As CEO of Pitney Bowes during that frightening time, Mike Critelli was charged with making the mail safer. He led the Mailing Industry CEO Council and came up with a private-sector solution for dealing with anthrax. Pitney Bowes created processes to scan mail safely when government mail room operators couldn't get it done.

"The anthrax situation was complicated," Mike said in our interview. "We already operated many federal government mail rooms, including in the House of Representatives. We had a four-pronged strategy for screening mail safely. First, move incoming mail processing off site. Second, use negative air pressure chambers to extract particles from the envelopes and quarantine the mail for four days. Third, offer to scan letters and send them electronically, a solution about one-third of House members accepted, which reduced risky mail. Fourth, get all our customers to do a risk-profiling of their mail so that they could spot suspicious letters and packages."

Leading through unexpected challenges is how leaders earn their pay. You're the one who has to keep the team focused and make sure you get the car back on the road and keep going. All eyes will be on you, whether things go right or wrong. You have to believe in the plan, project confidence, and lead decisively in the new direction. But if you don't have all the answers, it's okay to admit that. Don't deceive your people, or you'll damage their trust. They'll forgive you for not knowing everything, but not for lying to them.

Fortunately, there is a tool kit that you can open to help you lead effectively during times of uncertainty or crisis:

- The wrench in this tool kit is being solution oriented. After the explosion on board Apollo 13, when everyone was speculating and starting to panic, flight director Gene Kranz famously told his controllers, "Work the problem. Don't make things worse by guessing." In other words, focus on solutions, not damage control, not blame, not optics, and not figuring out what went wrong. Your best insurance against the unexpected is to have procedures in place for everything you can, and train on them until they are instinctive.
- The screwdriver in the tool kit is empowering your people to be problem solvers. We pay team members to run things and figure things out, not simply to take orders. The leader's job is to teach and train and instill confidence, then to step back and let people find solutions, even if it means accepting some failures. Strong employees don't want to sit back and be passive. They want to get their hands dirty, pitch in, and help fix things. This gives them a chance to show off their skills and resilience and also takes away a great deal of the fear around the unexpected.
- Your pliers are simplicity and clarity. Communicate early, often, and unambiguously. This makes it more likely that your initiatives will be embraced, practiced, and executed. The last thing you want is a game of telephone that breeds rumors, untruths, and fear. Who needs to know what's going on? Who

should you communicate with and in what order? How are you communicating? In person is often best, but not always possible, such as during a global pandemic, so Zoom, phone, or email become useful tools. Make sure the "why" of the new action is clear, not just the "what" and "how." Remember to allow for questions and feedback.

WHEN WE'RE AT OUR BEST

The funny thing about unexpected bumps in the road or big failures is that they can be blessings in disguise. They can show you who your stars are—your leaders, the fearless ones, the creative geniuses. Human beings are at our best when we're striving, out of our comfort zone, pushing to solve problems. Give your team room to show you what they can do when the chips are down, and they might amaze you.

For you, the leader, even the concern that you'll be caught by surprise by a reversal of fortune can make you better. If you worry that being unprepared will cost you your team's trust or some of your best people, you're more likely to be prepared. That "strategic anxiety" is a powerful tool for preventing complacency, but keep it to yourself. Never let your team see you sweat.

IN THE REARVIEW MIRROR

- The unexpected will upend your plans and goals.
- Great organizations adapt and keep going.
- Cultural resilience comes from defining the problem, generating alternatives, making decisions, and creating an

implementation process.

• Leading through the unexpected means being solution oriented, empowering people to be problem solvers, and fostering simplicity and clarity.

CHAPTER 8

THE DESTINATION IS JUST
THE BEGINNING

*Excellence means always looking for the next
destination, the next opportunity to create an amazing
outcome. Take ownership of culture, pursue excellence,
and never stop aiming for a higher standard.*

A
s you and your team get closer and closer to your destination,
you're going to learn a great deal. You're going to learn what
motivates your people and what demotivates them. You'll
also learn about capacities you had no idea your people pos-
sessed. This is a story about one of those surprises.

Way back when I was an assistant manager at one of the
Hartford stores, I worked with a man named Henry Robinson.
Henry was one of the nicest guys in the world, and while he wasn't
necessarily the most talented guy on my team he was an "attitude
and effort" employee—hardworking, positive, always ready to
pitch in. I would frequently spend extra time with him on training

when others assumed he couldn't do the job, and he became a good salesperson. I thought I knew who Henry was, but I would find out there was even more to him than I realized.

One day there was a gentleman in the branch who sent up red flags. It might have been his driving record, no auto insurance, a poor credit score, an address that didn't check out—there were a number of reasons our guidelines might flag someone as a poor risk. Anyway, we could not rent him a car, and when I explained this to him, he wasn't happy about it. I said, "I'm sorry, if there's anything else we can do, I'll even call one of our competitors," but he started yelling and calling me every name in the book.

The lobby was full of people, and this guy was escalating things. I was doing my best to control the situation, but I didn't have a lot of experience. All of a sudden, Henry walked over, as calm as Gandhi. What a lot of people didn't know about Henry, including me, was that he was a third-degree black belt in karate and a Gold Gloves boxer who had sparred with one of the top pro boxers of the day. Henry could handle himself and was very well known in the local community.

He came over and addressed the irate customer by name, and then calmly told him, "Let's discuss this outside, okay?" Just like that, Henry walked the customer out of the lobby, and they had a little chat outside for a minute or two. A couple of minutes later, as I was trying to get the lobby calmed down and get transactions moving again, the two men walked back inside. The irate customer walked up to me, calm and even a little embarrassed. Then he apologized to me for being rude and causing a scene and left quietly. I was shocked. But after that I always knew I could depend on Henry. There was a lot more to him than I realized.

PEOPLE CAN BE MORE THAN YOU THINK

There are two points to that story. First, loyalty matters. I had earned Henry's trust, and it paid off. As I like to say, "The more they trust, the harder you can push." Second, your people are probably capable of more than you—and they—imagine. Henry wasn't a rock star in terms of his performance at work, but he was strong, brave, confident, and calm, and those are incredibly valuable qualities when you're dealing with the public.

The men and women who make up your team probably have as much untapped capacity and hidden talent as Henry had, and maybe more. It's your job as the leader to create an environment of *elevation*, where individual contributors and managers can find the resources and coaching to develop those capacities and rise to the next level. It's your role to encourage them to never be satisfied and to seek constant improvement.

Yes, it's important to draw your road map and steer toward a destination, but that's today's journey. We don't stop there. We don't let complacency set in. Great organizations always have the next destination in mind, and they never, ever settle for "just okay" when they can elevate and pursue excellence. As the saying goes, "Winning wants all of you."

Maybe you and your team lead the pack in your particular state or region, and that's fantastic. Take time to high five and celebrate. But after that it's time to go for number one in the country, and in order to do that you must improve your plan. Not change the plan—just enhance the plan. Call an audible. Dish a behind-the-back pass. Reenergize the team. Keeping things fresh and exciting is critical in the elevation stage.

Do you know why it's so hard for a sports team to win back-to-back championships in any sport, from a World Series to an NCAA championship to a Super Bowl? Because complacency sets in. When you win, you rest on your laurels and stop doing what got you to the top. That's what made the University of Connecticut Huskies women's basketball team so incredible. They have consistently been the most successful women's basketball program in the nation, and at one point won a women's record four consecutive NCAA championships from 2013 through 2016, as well as setting the record for most consecutive wins in college basketball history by any team, men's or women's. They won 111 straight games, with the streak finally ending on March 31, 2017, when a buzzer-beater by Mississippi State at the end of overtime dealt them a 66–64 loss in the NCAA Final Four.

How did UConn do all that? For starters, it was leadership and an organization that consistently brought out the best in everyone. As a leader, let your team know you're not going to settle for good. You want them to be the best.

THE PLATEAU

A Japanese concept called *kaizen* reflects my approach to elevation and continually striving for more. The word means *change for better*, and this refers to businesses that intentionally work to improve in all their functions, from the supply chain to the sales process. Kaizen is now practiced worldwide but came to widespread attention as part of *The Toyota Way*, a set of ideals and methods that the Japanese car giant first published in 2001. In an organization that practices this philosophy, even small, incremental improvements are critical because they keep you moving forward and finding new ways to become more efficient, more productive, and more service oriented.

I discovered the importance of continuous improvement during a challenging period in my region. Several years after I became regional VP, I faced an unexpected and concerning trend: Our customer service scores, one of the core areas of our business and an area in which we had always excelled, suddenly flatlined, and we were on the verge of dropping below the corporate average. That's a big problem when "Customer service is our way of life" is one of your company's core values. Also, one big promotional criterion for our managers was that you didn't qualify for a promotion if your team's customer service score was below corporate average. That meant that for the first time my list of employees who were ineligible for promotion was growing. The timing for this couldn't have been worse. We were heading into our busy summer season, during which our customer service scores historically flattened anyway. Employees would be taking vacations, which would put pressure on the team. We had lost some key people to promotions, so our bench would be tested. Finally, a new and highly anticipated internet-enabled tablet that was supposed to make customer transactions faster and smoother, was turning out to be confusing and frustrating. Our inability to quickly master this device, which was supposed to shorten our transaction time and improve the customer experience, was having the opposite effect. And the technology wasn't going away. We had mothballed our old desktop computers and had gone all in on wireless technology. We had to make it work, and we were failing.

I did something that was unusual for me: I scheduled a branch manager meeting on short notice and ran the entire thing. Prior to that meeting, I met with my regional manager, HR manager, and talent acquisition manager, and we generated a few key moves for some of our challenges. While we normally discouraged our branch managers from playing the "I need more people" card, we had to admit that the busy summer season and a spike in our employees being promoted to other regions justified additional bodies. We decided we would add seven more interns than the previous year and position them at our high-profile stores, and we would start intern training several weeks earlier.

Also, before the meeting, my regional manager reached out to a few of our top performers in customer service and asked them to be prepared to talk about how their teams used our technology to create a more efficient customer experience. The only responsibility the other managers had before the meeting was to respond to a survey with the top three reasons why they felt our service levels had become stagnant and some possible fixes.

At that meeting I told my managerial team how concerned and disappointed I was, starting with myself. I made it perfectly clear that this performance wouldn't be tolerated. We had to solve these problems; however, I also knew this was a huge coaching opportunity. I then shared the results of the manager survey, which in overwhelming fashion pointed to the challenges with the technology and the confusion of the features and benefits. Our team was on to something. After a thirty-minute demo from our key ambassadors on the best way to utilize the technology, we realized the focus was on the wrong features. We then committed to having goals for each feature and tied in the usage of the technology to become a requirement in order to be recognized for the branch with the best customer service. At the end of the meeting, we recapped everything, sent a follow-up email to all the management, and gave a small homework assignment. Each manager would discuss the features, benefits, and goals we committed to during their next morning huddles as well as including this topic at their next mentor meeting.

My regional manager also had a homework assignment. Over the coming weeks, he would fine-tune our customer service training program so all levels would be aware of the recent enhancements. With a strong understanding of how to use the technology, and important buy-in from our key voices within the region, our team quickly got more comfortable with all the key features and benefits of the device. As confidence grew, so did our usage. The more we used it the more we got excited about its features. The excitement became contagious; everyone wanted to one-up the neighboring store by sharing success stories. The transformation was incredible.

Next thing we knew, our marketing improved, as everyone suddenly realized this technology gave us a distinct advantage over our competitors. The next step was clear: we needed to blitz the marketplace and tell everyone! Bottom line: When we mastered its functionality, sales went up by 20 percent because our employees were creating a more memorable experience. Even better, our service score improved by 7 percent during our most high-volume time. This is a great example of the ripple effect of culture and how it spreads to other areas.

This process was one I've detailed throughout this book and have used throughout my career. It was one of the main ingredients in our secret sauce, and I call it The **H-our-glass**:

1. Discovery. When you and your leadership team are all reporting similar, serious issues that are affecting the execution of your road map—what I called "commitments"—from sources such as field visits and regular phone calls, your first step should be to get together and compare your findings and thoughts. This is where

you will identify recurring patterns that require immediate action.

2. Orchestrate the plan. Next, bring in a select group of mentors and leaders, such as my think tank, and orchestrate how you will collaborate to solve this major problem.

3. Rollout. Introduce your new initiative to your team comprehensively and transparently. Be clear on what they'll need to learn, expectations, goals, and how you hope the organization will benefit. There are two keys here. First, ensure there is a role and understanding for each level of management. This ensures the initiative gains traction and momentum. Second, find a way for this commitment to be woven into the fabric of the existing playbook. For example, our technology situation above would be touched on in our morning huddles, weekly customer service meetings, thirty minutes of fame sessions, and mentor meetings. Everything was very intentional.

4. Training. Using exercises, role play, and lots of repetition, run your managers through your training program, and when they've mastered the new material, turn them loose to train your frontline employees. When pertinent, include new initiatives in your existing training modules. Otherwise, you will lose an opportunity to reinforce the message and need to rely on on-the-job training. This step closes the loop.

5. Assessment. When it's time for your people to put the new training into action with customers, collect relevant data and watch closely to see what kind of results your new initiative yields in both the short term and long term. Accountability is key, so we would always include an important initiative on the performance review forms and observe behaviors during field visits and one-on-ones. Take every opportunity to reinforce VIP items.

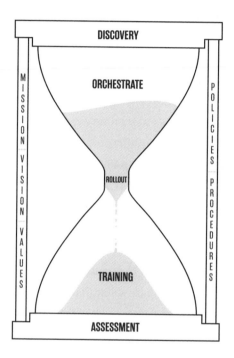

KNOW EVERYBODY'S UNIQUE STORY

While having a process like The **H-our-glass** in your back pocket is extremely useful, your solution for continually elevating and improving performance should be unique and targeted to your people and culture. One-size-fits-all solutions won't get it done. That means it's important to know your people, which brings us full circle back to listen, observe, and learn. Your people's motivations for improving will differ depending on their story. That's why you should know their story and personal background and understand what makes them who they are.

That's why, for me, those thirty minutes of fame one-on-one sessions were so important to fostering an environment in which people weren't just *willing* to improve but *wanted* to. The great thing about those half-hour face-to-face chats between branch managers and individual contributors was that they really let our branch managers get to know their employees as people. They were wonderful ways to get to know everyone's unique character and strengths. A manager might come away thinking, *Okay, this woman's ability to connect with people is extraordinary. I want her to be customer facing,* or, *this guy has a brilliant analytical mind. I need him laser focused on data collection and analysis.*

The better my managers and I knew our employees the better we could set them up to be successful with our improvement initiatives. If you want to speed to your destination in style, start by learning your people's strengths. Learn what makes them who they are.

⬆ ROADSIDE ATTRACTION

Change isn't the same as improvement. This story, which is satirical but accurate, illustrates why. Years ago an American corporation and a Japanese corporation decided to stage a canoe race on a great American river. Both teams trained exhaustively, and when the day of the race came the Japanese team won by a mile. The embarrassed Americans formed a commission to investigate why they had lost.

After six months, the commission issued its report: the Japanese team had won because it had seven paddlers and one person steering, while the Americans had two paddlers and six people steering. Knowing they needed to change in order to beat the Japanese in a rematch, the Americans reorganized. Now they would have four steering supervisors, two area steering superintendents, and one assistant superintendent steering manager.

At the rematch, this left one paddler in the American boat. The Japanese team won by five miles. The American company laid off the paddler, sold the canoes, and defunded the entire paddling research program. The Japanese kept doing what they had been doing all along: reducing the friction of their canoes and practicing paddling in unison.

The moral: not all "improvements" are improvements.

ENGAGEMENT AND BURNOUT

The meetings, one-on-ones, trainings, and sessions in the field had an important underlying purpose: They ensured a high level of employee engagement. Continually pushing for improvement asks a lot of employees, and I wanted to ensure I was always balancing my people's needs with the needs of my region. Engaged employees have higher job satisfaction, deliver better results to your customers and accounts, and over the long term keep the business ahead of the competition.

To facilitate this, I would set up my meetings and trainings in a way that satisfied the five factors of engagement:

1. A strong relationship with your manager. I wanted a commitment from my managers to learning about their employees' goals, ambitions, and personal lives.

2. Clear communication of expectations and goals. The objective was awareness with no surprises or confusion, ensuring our processes and procedures were in alignment.

3. The right materials, equipment, and information to achieve desired outcomes. Give people what they need to succeed. This might range from the technology to lifelong training.

4. A manager who encourages personal and professional growth. This might mean helping an employee create an individual development plan, grow and sharpen their personal brand, improve work-life integration, or expand their support network.

5. A system in which top performance is recognized. This is where our bimonthly Club Elite dinners came from. Everything was about driving the right behaviors in order to get the right results.

When people have the tools and teaching they need to do their best work, get the opportunity to grow professionally, and have leaders who pay attention and care about them, they become engines of continuous improvement. These methods lead to higher employee engagement across all groups. Turns out all that talk you've heard about millennials not wanting to engage turns out to be hot air, says Tracy Maylett, the engagement expert.

"Engagement is actually tenure-based or career lifecycle-based," he said in our interview. "Have you noticed that you're reading a lot less about millennials in the workforce? There's a reason for that. Millennials now represent fifty-one to fifty-five percent of the workforce, and we're finding when we look at different age demographics that engagement is more based on career maturity than age demographic."

"I've been in my role for five years, for the next ten years I'm going to be focused on my growth," he continues. "Then, I might start saying, 'Why am I doing this?' Our research suggests that the huge difference between the generations is overblown. This is about tenure. It doesn't matter whether you're sixteen or sixty-five. If you stay with a company long enough, you'll go through the same transformational process." That's good news. It means the same basic engagement tools that work for your current employees will work for your future employees, no matter their age. Whether you've got millennials or zoomers on staff, you're covered.

Engagement is also a powerful burnout preventer. Burnout doesn't just happen because of overwork. It happens because people are bored, stuck, or in a rut. They might not see the greater purpose of their work, or they might be struggling due to a lack of training and guidance. That's why I challenged our people and tried to keep things fresh. I wanted people to learn something new all the time because that would keep them engaged. That's why, in my region, we tried to master the challenge mindset.

I love the analogy of each day as a round of golf. If you're playing golf and hit a poor shot or play a bad round, okay. But what did you learn from your round? How will you use it to improve your round tomorrow? Can you reflect on a few good shots that will keep you coming back? A tip someone gave you that will help in a future round? When my people went home for the day, I wanted them to be thinking, *I picked up something today that I'll use tomorrow to make things better*. It didn't matter how small the lesson was—small things add up.

The other thing we did that increased engagement and prevented burnout was empower our managers. If you were one of our managers, you had a lot of control over how you managed your business.

We taught managers to look at trends and needs, think outside the daily grind, and respond from a solution mindset.

We devised systems that gave managers a chance to say, "Time-out." What were their employees doing, and what *should* they be doing? Are the wrong people doing the wrong things? We would go over responsibility rosters together, and they would go over the talent playbook with their people. Our managers didn't need permission to write up a work schedule or train their people. With the exception of some hiring decisions, my managers ran their own show. They bought in, took ownership, and sank their teeth into the work. As a result, this limited burnout. Our managers enjoyed the fast pace—running and gunning with a busy office, a lot of customer traffic, and a great team around them.

This is the most important thing I've learned about burnout:

You can push your people to the level of training you've given them.

We were always cross-training. If I wasn't training the managers directly, I was listening in while my department heads trained them. We always had multiple levers moving and people learning in more than one way. The better you train people, and the more you empower them, the more they can do and the faster they will advance. That's great for everyone.

THE JOHN WICK SCHOOL OF MANAGEMENT

In the movie *John Wick*, there's a line: "I gave him an impossible task, a job no one could have pulled off." I took that as inspiration. I challenged my team, and we made bets every year with my department heads and area managers. If we hit a big goal, we got some really cool rewards, depending on the level of our performance. Let's say we ranked in the top ten on the corporate matrix, which ranks all the regions on the core areas of our business within the company—that would entitle us to go to a casino for a day of fun. Scoring in the top ten *and* winning an achievement award meant a two-day trip to wherever. If we got three marks of excellence, I would fly everyone to Florida, Las Vegas, you name it, for an all-expenses-paid Thursday–Sunday holiday—on me. I paid for those trips gladly. The stories and bonding that came from those trips were priceless.

People drive elevation and improvement, so they need motivation. I made sure my area managers, branch managers, and frontline workers knew that if we as a team did more and achieved big things, good stuff would follow. We would feel a sense of accomplishment. Everyone would earn more money. There would be recognition and opportunities for promotion. We would get to take a victory lap and drink from the Stanley Cup, so to speak. Never neglect motivation. While it's nice to think you'll only hire people with the same intrinsic drive you have, that's just not true. Most people need tangible reasons to keep improving. That's human nature.

For example, one year, as our region was coming down to the final months of our fiscal year, we noticed growth was an at-risk category we needed to improve in order to win a prestigious team award. We decided to assign every branch its own target growth number. If each branch hit its number, that would assist our region in achieving our team goal. This number was posted on the wall of the manager's office so everyone would know what they were shooting for. We wanted everyone to know they would personally play a key role in the region's success. Because the people on our team cared about each other, no one wanted to be the one who let the team down, keeping everyone from achieving the team's goal.

But there was more than regional pride at stake. When the region wins an award, other regions want the employees who are part of that high-performing culture. When employees get promoted, there's a ripple effect of new opportunities. More opportunities equal more excitement. More excitement equals stronger belief and sense of belonging. Stronger belief equals winning behaviors. Winning behaviors create momentum. Momentum amplifies your talent and culture.

It's also important to balance control at the corporate level with giving subordinates the freedom to create, improvise, take risks, and fail forward. If you have to choose between centralized and decentralized, your best solution is usually to hire great people, train them well, give them a road map, and then get out of their way. There are some other tools you utilize to advance both individual and team goals:

- Technology. Is there some tech that can help you be more efficient? Customer expectations are changing, and if you're not thinking of ways to enhance their experience you will fall behind. Look at what Uber, Airbnb, and Netflix have done.
- Mergers and acquisitions. There are times when it makes sense to join forces in order to strengthen a team. Think about Disney—their strategic move of joining forces with Pixar gave them access to the company's proprietary animation technology and allowed them to reach new heights.
- Reporting and data. Can your reporting be streamlined? Can it give you a clearer view of things and see unmet needs or opportunities waiting to be leveraged?

- Enhanced training. Is there a way to train more of your people faster, to make training more engaging, or to improve outcomes?
- Clearer, cleaner policies and procedures. Get out of your own way. Can something be tweaked to allow more flexibility and simpler execution?
- Loftier goals. Raise the bar. Ask more of your people, and you'll be surprised how often they'll give it to you.

As the leader, however, you don't get to focus exclusively on the reward. You've got to be thinking about the journey and the next destination. Over time, one of your goals should be to see the team become less motivated by money and rewards and more motivated by leveling up. Getting better and better should be its own reward. If you can infuse your culture with a sense of pride, you've hit a home run. Remember: you're like a personal trainer—it's your job to push your people and see the potential in them that they might not even see in themselves. They might dislike you for it at the time, but they'll love you when they see the results.

OFF-RAMP

In dealing with my region's troubling plateau in customer service, I dealt with the two kinds of change any leader must manage: inadvertent and intentional.

Inadvertent change is change forced on you by circumstances. When that happened to us, we were no longer among the company's elite in customer service. We had become ordinary. That's fine, but don't let your people start questioning the road map. Just because something goes wrong doesn't mean the playbook is invalid. It means stuff happens. Many times problems result not from flaws in the plan but from a lack of execution.

Intentional change is change you choose because things aren't working—our changes in how we handled our interns, for example. It allows people to have a voice and to prepare. The only caveat with intentional change is that you can't wait too long to initiate it when things are going south. Keep an eye on your numbers and your finger on the pulse of your team or organization so you know when to act.

CULTURE BEATS STRATEGY

Strategy is important, but it's only useful when you have good people executing it with alacrity, consistency, and attention to detail. When strategy fails, it's usually because the execution is poor. Having a strong culture built on training, values, and a hunger for excellence ensures solid execution. Culture is like a perfectly programmed operating system for your organization!

When I spoke with Tim Baxter of Samsung, he told me that he learned more in his first eighteen months at Samsung than he did in his last five years at Sony. They had the same clients and similar products, but the corporate cultures were totally different. Tim told me that Samsung's culture was one of never being satisfied. It was hyperfast, focused on continued improvement, and edgy, with a healthy touch of paranoia. "It was humbling," he said in our interview. "It was an environment you were excited to be part of, but you knew if you couldn't keep up with it, you'd be run over. It wasn't a culture for everyone."

Samsung demanded your best, and so did I and my team. Both organizations gave you what you needed to be your best, stood back, and let you make the call. If you could deliver, you'd be rewarded.

If not, you might get more training, but you might also get a whack with the velvet hammer, a compassionate but firm correction making it crystal clear that you needed to do better, starting *now*.

Stuart Udell, CEO of Achieve 3000, which offers cloud-based solutions that accelerate and deepen learning in literacy, math, science, and social studies, says that culture beats strategy, but that the relationship between the two needs to be symbiotic. Culture should power strategy, and strategy should reinforce culture. "Otherwise, you can have an engaged workforce and still lose $80 million," he said in our interview.

I couldn't agree more. A culture of continuous improvement is the result of a lot of factors: sound strategy, a deep commitment to training and coaching, and an equally strong commitment to helping employees reach for excellence—when possible, for its own sake.

IN THE REARVIEW MIRROR

- Leaders should never be satisfied with the status quo but always looking to pursue excellence.
- People can have an unexpected capacity to achieve extraordinary things.
- The Japanese concept kaizen reflects the drive for continuous improvement.
- The **H-our-glass**: a five-part process for improvement.
- Know the unique story of everyone on your team.
- Engagement is the remedy for burnout.
- You can push your people to the level of their training.
- Culture really does beat strategy, but the two should be symbiotic.

CHAPTER 9

CHECK UNDER THE HOOD

*In igniting a winning culture, you don't need to
discard every aspect of your current culture. It is
possible to measure culture to see what's working and
what isn't.*

I n 2019 researchers from universities in Ohio, Canada, and
Hong Kong published the results of an experiment. They had
attempted to measure corporate culture using a form of artificial intelligence called machine learning. Using sophisticated
algorithms to analyze the words used in earnings calls with
shareholders and reporters, the researchers were able to determine that a strong culture was associated with greater operational
efficiency, more corporate risk-taking, executive compensation
that encouraged risk-taking and long-term thinking, and a higher
company value. They also found that the link between culture and
performance was more obvious in difficult times and that companies
whose cultural values were aligned were more likely to merge.

WHAT'S ON THE BUMPER STICKER?

BE MINDFUL OF HOW YOU COMMUNICATE

One thing I would personally recommend for your own self-evaluation is to review the last five emails in which you communicated an important message to your team. Was your message and direction clear? How was your tone? What were the common words used? Was it professional? Should it have been a phone call?

A corporate culture is a shared system of behaviors, values, and norms that define how people think, feel, and act, and that can seem like a nebulous, impossible-to-measure thing. But that's not true. You can measure culture, and what's more, it's imperative to do so. Throughout the course of this book, I've taken you on a road trip of sorts, a journey from my early days in corporate America to today, and along the way we've looked at the key components to a successful organizational journey: listening, learning and observing, laying out a clear road map, providing extensive training and coaching, and more.

But we haven't addressed the question of what you do when you've packed the car, chosen your fellow travelers, assigned someone the responsibility of overseeing the music, figured out where you are on the map, and set off down the highway. How do you keep an eye on your culture to make sure it's still in shape to get you to your destination? Is it even possible to do that?

I think you can, and that's important because there might be some aspects of your current culture that work well. When you're trying to give your organization an edge, you don't want to throw the baby out with the bathwater. When I became regional VP, I took over a struggling culture. But that did not mean everything needed unwinding. There were a few things that just needed some fine-tuning. The company still had an amazing product, and we had some amazing people. We just had too much noise. There were threads of greatness at work, there were people who I knew could become culture carriers, and there were systems and plans that had the potential to work very well with the right adjustments.

The point is that in optimizing your culture for the journey ahead, you do *not* have to build from scratch. But you are always one or two bad decisions away from losing momentum, so you should always be on guard, even if you have a really good culture. Keep in mind what Jim Collins, the famous author of *Good to Great*, called the Stockdale Paradox: you must maintain unwavering faith that you can and will prevail, regardless of the difficulties, while having the discipline to confront the most brutal facts of your current reality. Even as my team went through our evolution, I always managed with a healthy fear of what might go wrong. We had to stay on top of where we were headed and constantly be looking to the future.

A STRONG CULTURE IS OBVIOUS

Measuring culture is a matter of measuring quantitative results—things like profit, growth, retention, and customer service scores—and also finding a way to measure qualitative metrics, such as communication, favorable policies and procedures, leadership, work ethic, flexibility, accountability, and opportunities for advancement. Combine the quantitative and qualitative measures, add some of your own judgment and experience based on your observations, measure against the last set of data, and you'll know whether your culture is getting stronger or weaker.

A strong culture keeps your people engaged and wanting to stay with your company, focused on doing great work and meeting higher and higher expectations, all while staying in alignment with the company values and mission. A positive culture keeps revenues, profits, and market share growing. It's an energy source, and it's contagious. Remember culture carriers? When your culture is running clean and smooth and barreling down the road at eighty-five with the windows down, you can feel it. Everyone becomes a culture carrier. It feels great to come to work, and you and your team feel like a finely tuned machine.

A weak culture is just as obvious, and the symptoms are everywhere. Employees are confused, angry, or apathetic. Expectations are unclear, training and development are lacking, follow-through and accountability are nonexistent. It appears as if every initiative is the flavor of the week. Nobody knows what the company vision is, so there's no clear direction. While some good people get promoted, others become frustrated and leave. Work is inconsistent, as is customer service, because your people aren't pulling together. Instead of being united by a single clear "this is who we are and what we stand for" idea, they're fragmented. It's "every employee for themself."

A MOVING TARGET

Measuring culture may sound reductive, but it's not. In fact, it's necessary. Culture is a complex system and a moving target, and if you want to stay on top of how your culture is developing and changing, as well as areas where you might be falling short, then you need a way to measure the health of your company's culture.

David Pachter of JumpCrew, in talking about the challenges of coming back from remote work after the pandemic, said the experience has shown him that maintaining culture is a full-time investment of resources and attention. "The thing that really stood out coming out of 2020 was how hard culture is to maintain and how intentional you need to be about your investment of time and resources," he said in our interview. "The commitment needs to come from the top. You can't just hire a director of learning and development and think that you've covered your bases. You need a holistic, integrated, intentional program that fits with your culture and whatever your goals are. It's also not inexpensive."

As you look at optimizing your culture to be the best it can be, keep what works even as you change or discard what doesn't. The only way you'll know what works is by getting data—measuring your culture. So, as we wrap things up and I leave you to continue your journey with hope, a good map, and a great road trip playlist, I want to share with you my insights on determining what works in your culture and what doesn't. The check under the hood process has four parts that you can adapt to your own unique situation:

1. Identify and understand the key parts of your culture.

2. Watch for warning lights on the dashboard.

3. Perform diagnostics to figure out what's not working.

4. "Check under the hood" to repair and renew the engine of your organization.

1. KEY CULTURAL PARTS

Every organization is different, but any group of people brought together for a common purpose will share some of the same cultural pieces. This is the spectrum of cultural parts I've observed over the years. I've listed them in order from the easiest pieces of a culture to change to the ones I believe are the most challenging:

- Procedures—Workplace safety, opening and closing, promotional processes.
- Policies—Remote work and hybrid work, dress code, travel policies, social media accountability, you name it.
- People—Your methods and systems for teaching employees at every level, helping them reach their potential, and holding them accountable.
- Products—Not only what you sell but how it's designed, made, and maintained, and your supply chain.
- Customers—How you manage customer relationships, changing your target audience, as well as strategies for providing customer service.
- Technology—Your IT backbone but also technology enabling

everything from sales tracking to remote work to customer service.

• Mission—Why are you in business, and why does your company do what it does?

• Values—What ideas and virtues drive you, your people, and your behavior?

Changing procedures, even those in place for years, is a matter of developing new ones, training your people on them, and repeating the training until their performance is consistent. My leadership team and I did this sort of thing continually. We met every quarter and looked for trends in sales, customer service, and other areas. If we saw a trend that concerned us, we would keep an eye on it, communicate a reminder to the team at the affected branch, and if needed, change how our people did things.

On the other hand, instituting a new customer relationship management (CRM) system, like Salesforce, to replace your outdated one might be a great idea because your old system is keeping you from reaching revenue goals, but that kind of company-wide technology switch can be disruptive and costly. You'll meet with resistance at higher levels. It's also important to factor in the reality that some people fear change and will dig in their heels no matter how much sense your changes make.

Even more challenging are personal, moral, and ethical issues, such as a company's mission or values. What should your organization stand for? What should its mission be? Does its current mission make sense? If you ask one hundred people in your organization these questions, you will get one hundred different answers. One person's core ethical value might be insignificant to someone else. That can make cultural changes in these areas complex, requiring great care and discretion. Changing a company's moral and ethical compass requires a great deal of time, deliberation, and care, which is why you don't see organizations do that sort of thing very often.

But when a company does make a major change to one of its key cultural parts, the impact can be striking. Take Dick's Sporting Goods. After the February 2018 mass shooting at Marjory Stoneman Douglas High School in Parkland, Florida, the company removed all guns and ammunition from more than four hundred of its stores, and even destroyed $5 million worth of assault-style rifles. Dick's caught a ton of flak for its decisions from gun rights advocates, including boycotts, but they stood their ground. Following your moral compass can be costly in the short run, but it defines who you are as a company. According to *Fast Company*, while the company estimated that the decision to stop selling automatic weapons cost them over $200 million, the move eventually began to pay off as revenue rose close by 10 percent in 2020, and by the second quarter of 2021 sales were up 21 percent over the same quarter in 2020.[15]

If your organization changes its mission or values, its behavior must also change. For example, has pressure from employees forced your organization to be more aggressive in its efforts to combat climate change? That means you'll have to change how you operate, from where you get your electricity, to how you source your raw materials, to how executives travel to meetings and conferences. Changes to values and mission are fundamental changes to corporate DNA, which is why they are on the difficult end of my list.

Changing or upgrading cultural parts can be disruptive but transformative. That's what Melissa Wood, executive director, Cultural

---

15   Talib Visram, "How Dick's Sporting Goods went from championing gun reform to saving public lands," *Fast Company*, December 9, 2021, accessed April 4, 2022, https://www.fastcompany.com/90694388/how-dicks-sporting-goods-went-from-championing-gun-reform-to-saving-public-lands.

and Change Management, of CVS Health, told me about the efforts of Karen Lynch, the company's new president and CEO. "Karen is really investing in culture," Melissa said in our interview. "She wants to set the tone, make it feel different, and help our company move progressively into the future and be more innovative. One of the key things she's talking about is elevating some of the elements of our culture that are most important to us. We have five values, and underneath those are thirteen behaviors. But Karen has identified three things that are really important. I think we're probably going to dismantle some values and behaviors and go after our North Star. She's building our brand through culture."

"It's a brave new world," Melissa continues. "We have to be simpler, I think, in order to stay competitive and rally three hundred thousand troops in a really complex organization. The goal is to try to keep some things familiar but elevate them to priorities."

Are you familiar with your organization's key cultural parts? Can you list them in order of how difficult it would be to alter them? If you haven't done that exercise yet, try it now.

2. WATCH FOR WARNING LIGHTS

Once you know the parts that combine to form your culture, you need to start monitoring them as a way of monitoring the overall health of your organization. You keep your eye on your culture in the same way you would watch the key indicators of an automobile's condition on a long drive.

When you're on a long road trip, from time to time it's wise to pull over and check the oil and the tire pressure, watch the temperature gauge to make sure the radiator isn't overheating, and watch for those cryptic little warning lights in the shape of an engine, Aladdin's lamp, a battery, and so on. You don't raise the alarm unless something's really wrong, but you stay vigilant, and if something looks dicey—an unusual drop in tire pressure, for example—you'll pull over to see if something needs fixing.

You should be doing the same thing with the culture of your company, department, region, or team. This might be no more complex than listening to and observing how the social and collaborative dynamic of your team plays out. For Jeff Hayzlett of the C-Suite Network, the emotional state of the corporate community is an important indicator of its success or failure.

"Mood plays a big part in the culture of a company," he said in our interview. "What is the prevailing mood? If you have a bad mood, even though you've got a great product, you've got a problem. Let's say you're a restaurant with great food, but everybody's kind of arrogant. It doesn't make a difference what the food is like. But you can go to a dive restaurant where the staff is personable, and everybody has a great time."

Take your organization's pulse regularly and organically. This is about feel and instinct—think of it as adjusting the climate control during a long drive. You're walking the floor, holding one-on-ones, and so on. Communicate and encourage managers or other direct reports to do the same, and then download everyone's information in regular meetings or conference calls. What's going on? What's standing out? What are people talking about, complaining about, happy about?

Our Monday conference calls allowed me and my regional managers to receive a brief update on initiatives with my area managers, and we would include a rotating department head in the call. This helped keep our one-off initiatives top of mind so we could address any issues before they became problems.

Culture is not opaque. Because culture is a collection of behaviors, norms, and values, there are predictable telltales you can look for. When my team or I made branch visits, we might notice the store's level of preparation, the employees' energy, or if the attitude of some individuals was off, and this would tell us things were not going in a great direction.

Keep your eye on your culture's *artifacts*, which are those special "inside" attributes—an internal secret vocabulary, signals, jokes— that only people who are part of the tribe understand. Every organization has them. For instance, in my region, if an employee made an additional sale while outside with a customer—getting the person to upgrade to a more expensive vehicle, perhaps—when they came back into the branch, they would click their clipboard to tell the team, "I just helped boost our numbers," and get a quiet high five.

If we really wanted to be creative, the location might have an actual WWE (World Wrestling Entertainment)-style championship belt for the king or queen of sales or service. Catchphrases, our dress code, the cleanliness of our stores, the greeters who always welcomed our customers, little "CC-isms"—we had all sorts of unique artifacts that made us 24CC. They were part of the customer experience and the employee experience.

If those artifacts decline or disappear, that could also be a red flag for a culture in rough shape. That's something you might need multiple observations to notice because you have to get to know people's patterns. But after a while, when you know your people well, a bad attitude or disengagement stands out like a lighthouse on a dark night. Remember what I said earlier: if things aren't being done right while you, the boss, are watching, then you can be sure they are never done right.

There's one more important cultural touchstone many organizations overlook: *vendors and major accounts*. These are essential components of your business, and if they are leaving you or not communicating as well as they have in the past, something might be up with your company. Our vendor and account relationships were critical, and keeping those relationships strong was one of the factors that helped us weather the Great Recession of 2008. Our vendors and big corporate accounts knew we were still the same organization, rain or shine, and they trusted us.

Bottom line: there are consistent warning signs that a culture is losing its ability to motivate people or help them feel connected to each other and the organization. This is why listen, observe, learn is the most valuable advice I could ever give you. Just paying attention to small interactions and minor mistakes can give you valuable information you can use to make modifications in your culture before it reaches the crisis point. But even when you recognize there's a problem with your culture, you won't repair it without first knowing what aspect of your culture has stopped running smoothly. That's where diagnostics come into play.

3. DIAGNOSTICS

Soliciting the views of your managers and other leaders is one way to know which pieces of your culture aren't working optimally, but there are others. Every organization should have in place a process to continually check on its culture's health and vitality. Constant monitoring tells you when important cultural indicators start to decline so you can act preemptively rather than calling 911 when things go bad and some of the damage is already done. Just like with our cars, part of running diagnostics is a way of assessing its health, and the same can be said for company culture.

Having empirical information empowers you to act. It would be arrogant and dangerous of us to dismiss that. So we never dismissed it.

This is the diagnostic system for culture scoring I've been telling you about called the six-point inspection. A few thoughts before we get started. First, I've kept the system as simple and clear as possible because if something isn't simple and clear it's not sustainable. Second, doing regular assessments of your culture can seem like a heavy lift for leadership. You'll get better buy-in on making such assessments a permanent part of your culture if you talk about them in your annual performance reviews.

THE SIX-POINT INSPECTION

I call this system the six-point inspection because you're collecting data from six critical components that reflect what's happening inside and outside the company, like the multipoint inspection auto dealers perform on pre-owned cars. These are the different areas in which I recommend gathering data and how often I suggest doing so. Also, this is a weighted-scoring system, so some metrics are more important than others. While some companies may look at each one of these components separately, very few are looking at all six components together when assessing the health of the organization's culture. Each has a very important impact on igniting a high-performance culture. To be a standout organization, you can't rely on just one or two parts—you need them all working together, not in isolation. An engine doesn't run on just one component. It needs a variety of factors to drive you forward.

GATHERING YOUR SIX-POINT INSPECTION DATA

After each critical component, I've included how to gather and score the data for each one. Each one works on a 0–100 percent scale, except for profit and growth, which I'll get to. If you choose to do so, you could also break down each result, except profit and growth, by age, ethnicity, gender, or any other factors that suit your objectives.

These are the six critical components:

A. Engagement: Engagement is critical, and annual employee engagement surveys can't capture every facet. Anonymous quarterly engagement surveys are the gold standard here. Tracy Maylett, whose company has collected a database of about fifty million engagement surveys, backs this up. In our interview, he talked about the "I'm just grateful to have a job" factor as one possible factor that caused engagement scores to rise while people were working from home during the pandemic.

But further research revealed that while that was a minor factor in higher scores what really drove engagement higher was intentionality: managers and executives being conscious and intentional about showing up, communicating, and engaging with individual contributors in a way they didn't have to when everyone was in the office. When my engagement results were high, it usually indicated my retention numbers were about to improve. Conversely, when my engagement numbers were low, even if my retention was presently strong, I was about to see a dip. Pay close attention to the relationship between the two. According to Gallup's 2020 Q^{12}® Meta Analysis, there is a strong relationship with employee engagement at work and organizational outcomes. As a matter of fact, when comparing organizations in the top half quartile to those in the bottom quartile, the study showed significant differences in profitability (23%) and productivity in sales (10%).[16]

Gathering engagement data: Conduct a survey of eight to twelve questions using the Likert scale, but on the scale from "agree completely"—employees who go beyond their job description—to "agree somewhat"—employees who are strong and steady and do what's asked—to "not sure," to "disagree somewhat"—employees who suffer in silence and are passive—to "disagree completely"— unconscious or conscious sabotage. Examples include:

- I would recommend our company to my friends as an employer.
- I receive the support I need from my manager.
- I am proud of the work I do at the company.

Add the average percentage of "agree completely" results to get your engagement score. For example, if an average employee answers four out of twelve questions "agree completely," then your engagement score is 33. For all surveys I suggest having a firm that specializes in such surveys prepare, administer, and tabulate them for you. They know all the most effective questions, not to mention that a survey from a third-party firm seems more objective to your people.

---

16   Gallup, "Gallup Q^{12}® Meta Analysis," Gallup, n.d., accessed January 25, 2023, https://www.gallup.com/workplace/321725/gallup-q12-meta-analysis-report. aspx.

B. Customer satisfaction: Everything we did centered on improving the customer experience, and the heart of the data gathering was the overall satisfaction ranking given by our customers upon the completion of the transaction. If you prefer to use Net Promoter Score, that's fine. But you should always be gathering data on how your customers feel about their experience: employee behavior, product quality, speed, convenience, etc. Tabulate that data quarterly and look for patterns:

• Groups with scores much higher or lower than the average. Superstars could be carrying your team, department, or organization, while poor performers could be dragging you down.
• Dips or spikes in your overall scores. Spikes are great, but are they flukes, or do they represent genuine improvement? If the latter, how can you catch that lightning in a bottle?

Also, don't limit yourself to internal customer service comments. I would have my executive assistant monitor review sites, such as Yelp and Google, searching for obvious patterns, good and bad. Doing this allowed me to recognize problems: behaviors or values being compromised, branches falling short in their numbers, employees who were recurring problems, and common themes among customer complaints.

If the data revealed a trend that needed correction, I got my leadership team together to discuss how operations needed to change. I let my department heads know they were also accountable for the customer service scores of each branch, not just the managers of those branches. In the end, we came up with "teams." I had department heads pick a handful of branches that they "owned." They would be debriefed before going into the field to communicate our regional customer service commitments. In essence, they acted as a support and coach for their branches, and at times they would even roll up their sleeves and assist with customers. After each visit, they would share feedback and provide tips as well as communicate their findings to the appropriate levels.

Nine department heads would cover all branches. This helped the people working at the branches feel like someone cared, and it brought everyone together. We even gave a reward to the department head whose teams showed the greatest improvement, which helped create an atmosphere of pride instead of a "that's not my job" mentality. There is also an additional ripple effect when the engagement of your employees also benefits and changes the experience of both clients and customers. Indeed, according to Gallup, "Fully engaged customers represent a 23% premium in share of wallet, profitability, revenue, and relationship growth over the average customer."[17]

Gathering customer service data: Conduct a one-question survey—"How satisfied are you with our company's customer service?"—using the typical five-point Likert scale: completely satisfied, moderately satisfied, neutral, moderately dissatisfied, completely dissatisfied. The percentage of "completely satisfied" responses is your score. If 82 percent of customers respond "completely satisfied," your score is 82 percent. A key component to all surveys is giving the individual taking the survey an opportunity to write in feedback and expand on a point for each question that's asked. This is extremely valuable and allows for you and your team to pinpoint specific patterns that need sharpening.

---

17 Gallup, "Customer Centricity," Gallup, n.d., accessed January 11, 2023, https://www.gallup.com/workplace/311870/customer-centricity.aspx.

C. Cultural values: Your organization likely has a set of guiding values and ethics that define its culture. The question is, are the organization's actions and choices guided by those values? Employees respect an organization whose leaders take its core values seriously, but failing to do so—or adopting cosmetic values for the sake of appearances and then disregarding them—leads to cynicism.

My team created awareness of our values through endless reinforcement. At a new hire lunch, one of the first things I would do was hand new employees a sheet listing the company's founding values and briefly discuss how those values shaped the behaviors of the team. On day one they had that information. Later, in order to take some of the earlier tests for advancement, employees had to answer written and verbal questions about our values. In-house surveys would quiz employees on our value statement, including trick answers, like "We try harder," which was the slogan of one of our competitors.

If I was interviewing an internal candidate for a position, I would ask, "What are our founding values?" In training, we would start by going over our founding values.

As for ethics, they have become especially important in a post-pandemic world. Employees, especially younger workers, want to be part of an organization that tries to do the right thing and succeeds more often than not. Like it or not, today's companies are called on not only to be centers of economic growth but of moral authority.

In surveying your people on your organization's values and ethics, you're asking about consistency and authenticity. Are your company values clear? Do they reflect the company's mission in the world? Do your people feel your actions are consistent with those values? Are the guiding values reflected in everyday decisions and policies?

Gathering values and ethics data: As with engagement, this survey should feature eight to twelve questions about your organizational values, using the Likert scale from "agree completely" to "disagree completely." Sample questions include:

- "The actions of leadership reflect the company's stated values."
- "The organization applies its values consistently across all areas of the business."

The average percentage of "agree completely" responses is your values score. For example, if the average employee answers eight out of twelve questions "agree completely," then your values score is 66.

D. Diversity, equity, and inclusion (DEI): As society's attention has turned to very important issues, like gender identity and racial justice, organizations have been expected to keep up—to become more welcoming to people of all sexual orientations, all ethnicities, all gender identifications. Again, younger workers are particularly sensitive to such issues, and they can be the guiding light for leaders trying to determine what they're doing right and what they need to improve upon. We have the ability to create psychological safety in which all employees can demonstrate their unique skills and talents and truly feel not only valued but embraced.

I worked hard to improve DEI in my region, launching the Minority Interactive Network and Women's Interactive Network to serve the needs of people of color and women and help attract, retain, and advance a diverse workforce. In this area, action is everything. If your organization doesn't yet have programs to address diversity, equity, and inclusion, your employees are sure to insist on them—or they will leave for other organizations that take their concerns seriously.

WHAT'S ON THE BUMPER STICKER?

EVALUATE YOUR OWN CIRCLE

I would recommend also doing a self-assessment of your own personal and professional DEI circle. How diverse are your LinkedIn connections or Facebook friends? What about your dentist, physician, plumber, attorney, or accountant?

One way to incentivize your leaders to take DEI seriously is to incorporate it into your compensation and advancement plan. For example, maybe you cannot apply for a promotion unless DEI in your department meets certain targets.

Compile your DEI data in two ways:

1. To assess diversity, look at your hiring patterns in your metropolitan statistical area (MSA). I would compare the percentage of people of color and women we had hired to the percentage of people of color and women living in our MSA. This was a reliable predictor of how well we mirrored the communities we served.

Gathering diversity data: First, calculate your diversity score using your MSA findings. Just look at the percentage of people over the age of twenty-one who live in your MSA and determine what percentage of them are women or people of color. This data is easy to get by contacting the US Census Bureau. Now look at the percentage of people in your workforce who are women or people of color, and compare the two numbers. Your diversity score is the difference, expressed as a percentage, between the number of your employees who are women or people of color and the women and people of color who reside in your MSA. For example, if people of color and women make up 50 percent of the people over twenty-one in your MSA, and 40 percent of your company's workforce is women and people of color, your company is 80 percent as diverse as your MSA (40/50=80 percent). That's your diversity score.

2. Getting information about equity and inclusion means doing a straightforward survey. You're exploring people's concerns and then asking, "How well are we doing in this area?" Count on getting candid responses about a topic that many people feel strongly about.

Conduct a survey on equity and inclusion. As with engagement and values and ethics, this survey should feature eight to twelve questions, using the Likert scale from "agree completely" to "disagree completely." Sample questions include:

- "The organization has inclusive hiring, retention, and advancement policies."
- "The organization is a welcoming environment for people of different ethnicities, orientations, and creeds."
- "Are you able to bring up problems and tough issues?"

The average percentage of "agree completely" responses is your equity and inclusion score. For example, if the average employee answers nine out of twelve questions "agree completely," then your equity and inclusion score is 75 percent. Finally, average your diversity score and your equity and inclusion score. If your diversity score is 80, and your equity and inclusion score is 75, that's 155/2=77.5 percent. Rounding up, your DEI score would be 78.

E. Retention: In a labor market like today's, where people have lots of choices, they don't stay with a company where they're not engaged, enjoy their work, and have opportunities for financial reward and professional growth. If people are staying, and your retention numbers are solid, why? If they're leaving, why? This is where the "stay" interview I talked about earlier in chapter 5, as well as a good exit interview, are important. Don't treat the exit interview as a pro forma obligation; it can be a valuable way to find the leaks in your boat!

Look for the harbingers of turnover: employees falling behind on deadlines, poor performance, mentor program ineffectiveness, average hours worked, declining engagement scores, poor attendance at fun events, chronic absenteeism, especially on Mondays, 401(k) enrollment, and ethical hotline spikes.

By the way, if you have great camaraderie and energy, why not create a publicly accessible employee review and comment website—your own version of Glassdoor? If your people love your company that much, give them a way to spread the word that it's a great place to work to as many potential hires as possible.

Gathering retention data: Simply take the percentage of your people retained during the period you're reviewing. That's easy.

If you're like 24CC, you're around 80 percent.

F. Profit or growth: Profit is a clear metric of progress. What about growth? Well, growth can apply to revenue or market share because different metrics matter to companies at different stages. If you're an established company, profit will usually be your most important financial metric. But if you're a start-up, you might be more interested in growing or capturing market share, even if you're losing money right now.

Look at your profit or growth numbers for the most recent period and see how they compare with the same numbers for the corresponding period a year earlier—Q3 2021 versus Q3 2020, for example.

Keep in mind that spikes or dips can occur because of reasons that have nothing to do with your culture, such as the 2008 recession or the 2020 pandemic. But if the conditions for doing business are otherwise healthy and consistent, and you're still seeing a decline in profitability or revenue growth, ask yourself if the reason is poor performance.

When you look at sales, examine a variety of segments. Are you looking at one account or twenty? Is market penetration dropping with one group or several? Peel the onion and dig into all elements of your sales and revenue, not just the bottom line.

Gathering profit and growth data: We handle profit or growth (P/G) differently from the other critical components because the numbers can vary wildly. For a long-established company, a 10 percent boost in profitability can be huge, while a growing young company might routinely see revenue jumps of 200 percent a year. First, decide which metric you're looking at: profit, revenue growth, or market share growth. Once you've done that, look at the data and go straight to your score:

Negative	P or G	Positive
0	0-5	0
1	6-20	1
2	21-35	2
4	36-50	4
5	50+	5

SCORING THE SIX-POINT INSPECTION

In scoring this system, you're trying to accomplish three things:

1. Create a baseline. You want to establish a quarterly foundational score for each critical component to compare future scores against. This will become important later. If you already have quarterly data for all these areas, go ahead and use it.

2. Set up future rankings. Once you have your baseline, you'll run the same numbers again in a quarter or a year. When you do, compare your current quarter against the same quarter of the prior year. When you do, you'll be rating your new scores against your most recent baseline numbers to check your progress. This will give you a snapshot of the health of your culture—your six-point inspection score. By the way, your most recent scores become your new baseline the next time you run the six-point inspection. Note: you could also run these numbers from quarter to quarter if you think enough will have changed in just three months to justify the time and cost.

3. Heat check. If any of these six areas is at least 5 percent lower than your current goals, stop what you're doing. This is a potential cultural emergency, and you should take a close look at it as soon as possible. It's also a danger sign if more than 20 percent of respondents answer "completely unsatisfied" or "completely disengaged" to your engagement and customer service surveys. When setting goals, the intent is to pick a number that is attainable but a bit of a stretch.

The key to the six-point inspection is comparing your past rankings against today's rankings.

SCORING SCALE

Negative	Scoring Scale	Positive
0	0-3	0
1	4-7	1
2	8-11	2
4	12-15	4
5	16+	5

Suppose your retention number one year ago was 80, and this year, when you run the numbers, you scored an 86. That's six points higher than the previous year, so your retention score is +1.

Important! Employee engagement and customer satisfaction are especially important criteria, so we weight them more heavily. Double your scores in those two categories.

Example: Last year your customer satisfaction score was an 81. This year it dropped to a 70. That's eleven points down, which would normally be a –2, but since this is customer satisfaction, your score becomes a –4.

Once you have your baseline, each time you run your numbers for the six critical components in the future, compare them with your previous numbers to get your plus or minus scores for each critical component. Add those scores, and you have your six-point inspection score (or 6PI score), which indicates the health of your culture. Here's an example for a hypothetical organization:

2022 Six-Point Inspection Scoring for Company X

Engagement in Q1 of 2021:		30
Engagement in Q1 of 2022:		38
Change:		+8
Engagement scores are doubled:		+4

Customer Satisfaction in Q1 of 2021:		82
Customer Satisfaction in Q1 of 2022:		76
Change:		–6
Customer Satisfaction scores are doubled:		–2

Cultural Values in Q1 of 2021:		70
Cultural Values in Q1 of 2022:		75
Change:		+5
Cultural Values score:		+1

DEI in Q1 of 2021:		78
DEI in Q1 of 2022:		70
Change:		−8
DEI score:		−2

Retention in Q1 of 2021:		80
Retention in Q1 of 2022:		86
Change:		+6
Retention score:		+1

Profit/Growth 2021–2022:		+22
Profit/Growth score:		+2

TOTAL SIX-POINT INSPECTION SCORE:
+4 -2 +1 -2 +1 +2
= +4

CULTURAL HEALTH DASHBOARD

This is the final result, translating your six-point inspection score into a dashboard light so you can see how healthy—or unhealthy—your culture is today and know what kind of action you need to take. Keep in mind that if you have a dysfunctional culture—and are well below your goals—even logging a score of +3 might still mean your culture has problems. In these cases, you're looking for the change over time. Conversely, you could be competing against excellent numbers and appear as if your culture is in trouble by logging an inside out score of –3. This is where the goals you've created are important. Anytime your quarterly numbers are right on point with your quarterly goals, even if the dashboard states you have an opportunity, you should be culturally okay.

As a reminder, any of the critical components that come in at 5 percent below your goal are a potential red flag, even if your overall score looks good.

Also, keep in mind this is a snapshot in time. Just because you have a healthy culture today, that doesn't mean you'll still have one in six months. That's why you track trends—so you'll know what's working and what's not. The dashboard colors:

- White light—a 6PI score of +4 or higher indicates an overall healthy culture that is thriving and should be exported to other parts of the company. Bottle that secret sauce!
- Green light—a score from 0 to +3 means your culture is humming along just fine. There's not a lot for you to do.
- Yellow light—a score of –1 or –2 indicates some issues that could be small but could turn into something big if not nipped in the bud. You should investigate.
- Red light—a 6PI score of –3 or lower is an emergency. Pull the car over and examine every aspect of your culture—something is very wrong.

You can also use this tool to assess the health of any one of the six critical components, independent of the others. For instance, if all your other indicators look good, but cultural values fall off a cliff at −5, you can address that area of your culture by itself—and you certainly should, because trouble in one area tends to spread to others.

Keep in mind that my goal is to give you a simple way to ignite a winning, high-performance environment. The purpose of the scoring system is to give you empirical data and help you spot warning lights quickly and relatively easily; however, if you find a red flag in one or more of the critical components, I've given you a full suite of tools and methods in this book you can deploy to correct problems with your culture.

Another important distinction of my approach is that the scoring system uses quantitative and qualitative data. It takes into account not only the behaviors, values, and norms of an organization but also the actual performance results in key areas of a business.

ASSESSING RESILIENCE

In chapter 7, we discussed resilience as a core attribute of a high-performance culture. In a volatile, politically divided, stress-laden world, it's critical that resilience be deeply ingrained into a culture. Disruptive, transformational events occur more frequently, and the 24/7 media machine amplifies events that would not have had major implications in years prior. Separating true threats and opportunities from false alarms is more challenging than ever.

In this environment, leaders must build resilience *and* navigate potentially divisive issues. Resilience is not driven simply by achieving a unified response but by successfully "threading the needle" between a compassionate, effective response to events and accommodating the full spectrum of views and opinions. How leaders speak and write matters, and because leaders are also at risk of stepping on metaphorical "land mines," language matters. Stakeholder responses are more rapid, more complex, more voluminous. Making sense of them is not only essential to building resilience—is not only more challenging—but also more critical than ever.

If, after completing the six-point inspection process, you still feel you need a deeper look into your organization's culture, consider assessing its resilience using a tool called CAFÉ (Cultural Analytics Framework Executed) from a company called MoveFlux. CAFÉ goes beyond traditional employee surveys that only give you a retrospective look at what your people are thinking and feeling. Instead, it uses language-processing algorithms and artificial intelligence to analyze publicly available social media posts, internal company emails, and other written communication sources and deliver relevant insights about what employees, customers, and people in the community are saying and feeling about your company.

Unlike surveys, CAFÉ is designed to capture relevant, quantifiable warning signals about your culture before they turn into embarrassing problems, expensive failures, or personnel losses. These "warning lights" often reside outside the organization and can be found through social and mass media that employees and their families consume or create every day and night, mostly outside work. Through predictive analytics, CAFÉ monitors, identifies, quantifies, and prioritizes the warning lights that determine how resilient your organization will be in the face of culturally stressful events, including

- changes in leadership,
- failure of an initiative or project,

- resignations of key personnel,
- potential mergers,
- potential layoffs,
- political or social upheaval, and
- natural disasters.

CAFÉ continuously monitors important data sources—both influential people and influential points of view—to detect patterns in language choices and determine which ideas are gathering momentum within your organization. This empowers leaders to preemptively develop responses that address employee needs and concerns, helping employees feel acknowledged and making everyone accountable for the culture.

You can find more information about CAFÉ at MoveFlux.com.

N
⬆ ROADSIDE ATTRACTION

When Texas enacted a controversial ban on most abortions, Marc Benioff, the CEO of Salesforce, tweeted:

"Ohana (a Hawaiian word meaning extended family) if you want to move we'll help you exit TX. Your choice," followed by a red heart, a symbol of love. This was an offer Marc made to help relocate employees out of Texas who had concerns about access to reproductive health care.

The tweet's impact calmed employees across the nation, not just Salesforce, and pioneered corporations trying to help their employees regardless of the company's political beliefs, like Amazon, Citigroup, and Yelp. It also has several linguistic aspects:

1. The comments were neutral and nonpartisan. He never mentioned the word abortion.

2. He empowered people and appealed to their sense of autonomy through the two words "your choice."

3. It had a red heart—a symbol of love.

Abir Bhattacharyya, co-founder of MoveFlux surveyed a statistically valid sample from different companies approximately eight months later to see if the tweet had a residual lift. Do you think the tweet helped companies in corporate America? Roughly 88 percent said yes, indicating that this language of inclusivity remained a powerful export of Salesforce culture over time.

4. REPAIR AND RENEWAL

Gathering data and using the six-point inspection system is a lot of work, but when you've gotten all the data and input you can, and you're certain some of your key cultural parts are cracked or missing, your next job is to communicate that to everyone. After that, you'll need to bring everyone up to speed on the changes needed to fix things and the ways you'll be monitoring progress once the changes are in place.

Culture is a human construct, and from time to time it needs to be refreshed. Why do great coaches lose their jobs after ten or fifteen years with the same team, even if they've won championships? Did the coach or manager suddenly forget how to lead a team overnight?

Of course not; however, any sports coach is the custodian of the team's culture, and after enough time passes that culture becomes stale and loses its power to motivate and inspire people. Culture in any organization thrives on a balance of consistency and repetition, with a splash of variety. You need consistency and repetition to keep expectations, behaviors, and attitudes in line with the organization's values. But people get bored. They get too comfortable. They need new challenges, new incentives, new types of training, and fresh goals.

One example of this was how I changed our performance meetings. We would typically hold one-on-one meetings to train personnel on their marketing efforts. But after a few years, the whole thing was starting to get dull; results were falling off. What's more, if you have five direct reports, that's five more meetings you had to fit into your schedule. After receiving consistent feedback about the true value of these performance meetings from many levels, we called an audible. We turned the individual performance meetings into collaborative team performance meetings, something our millennial employees became very enthusiastic about. With more people and the same amount of time, meetings became more like a high-intensity speed round. Communication was better, energy was better, and training was better.

Not only did we save our typical managers about four hours a month by eliminating unnecessary meetings but the new format was so successful that one of my colleagues exported the idea to our European operations in Germany, where it is still in use today.

The idea at this stage is not just to replace components for the sake of doing so but to introduce clearer or more engaging elements to your culture that have the potential to bring you closer to your long-term goals. For instance, you might redesign your training, like I did with the four personality types, to address declining sales or the rollout of our thirty minutes of fame concept, which was introduced in and refined during our think tank sessions.

Maybe you'll prefer weekly or biweekly conference calls, staff meetings, field presence, or something else. Create your own best practices. Improving retention might mean creating an effective mentor program, conducting "stay" interviews, doing timely reviews, reviewing training material for effectiveness, or changing your pay plan.

You could institute a new system of incentives and rewards. Suppose one of the issues affecting your culture is that your employees want the company to have a more visible, active social conscience. You could launch a series of initiatives that incentivize your people to create fresh ideas for helping underserved parts of your community—by raising funds for local nonprofits, perhaps, or volunteering to clean up streets or empty lots. Whoever comes up with the most creative, effective idea gets a reward. The payoff is clear: improved performance, improved engagement, reduced turnover, and doing the right thing.

If your repair work is successful, you could wind up with a renewed culture, like what Melissa Wood has at CVS. In speaking with me for this book, she told me about a surprisingly simple initiative that has powerfully enriched the company's culture and increased employee engagement. "It was one of the most basic things," she said in our interview. "Ten years ago, we put new badges on store employees. You've seen them in some CVS stores—a big white badge with a red heart that reads 'I can help.' Those three words dramatically changed what was possible for us. This simple note became important to the human being who was wearing it. That says something about our company. After ten years of complex to-do lists of things and pulling off the impossible, that simple little badge has had more impact than anything I've done in my career. It's a simple visual that indicates why we're all here."

That is a great example of taking action to repair culture: simple, easy to implement, and easy to track. Give your employees a cultural artifact that's immediately visible to them and to your customers, note the date it goes into effect, and watch the results. If retention or customer satisfaction numbers improve, you probably have a winner.

Another important part of the repair process is to challenge "we've always done it this way" thinking. Organizations become fossilized in the way they do things. A policy that's been in place for the last five years might go unquestioned, especially by newer employees, even if it makes no sense or is counterproductive. That's when you need to step in and ask, "Is this really accomplishing what we want it to accomplish?" Take remote work. An organization might have been vehemently opposed to people working from home before COVID-19, but maintaining that policy now may cost that organization good people. It's up to you to question if doing something "because we've always done it this way" is serving everyone's best interests.

Finally, everyone who wants to play a part in shaping a new culture should be able to. The best cultures I've observed were the ones that took into account everyone's opinion and everyone's voice when shaping the future of the organization. You don't know where the next brilliant idea is going to come from, and sometimes those ideas come from the people with the least experience, as they see things with the freshest pair of eyes. Anyone who wants to drive should get some time behind the wheel.

OFF-RAMP

What do you do when your entire culture isn't the problem but a subset of that culture is? For instance, what happens when one of the departments, divisions, or stores you're managing is delivering strong sales numbers but following few if any of the policies and procedures you've laid out in your road map? Changing your entire culture over one such group seems like an overreaction. That's why we have to acknowledge the existence of microcultures—cultures within cultures, in which people do things their own way, not yours.

A microculture is a collection of norms and processes maintained by a smaller group within a larger culture—a team, a department, even the staff at a store. They have their own rules, and those rules, norms, and beliefs determine their outcomes. There will always be pockets of people who want to do things their own way, and that's probably not intentional defiance. Instead, it's usually the result of leadership allowing people to take shortcuts because they're getting decent short-term results while skipping over important mandates because they're deemed too complicated, too hard, or don't seem to produce those same results.

Microcultures are rarely beneficial in the long run. For one thing, their existence can undermine your authority. If team X doesn't have to follow your playbook, why should anybody else? But the bigger reason is that their positive results usually aren't sustainable. How you get the numbers matters. When a microculture is struggling, yes, you need to step in and get everyone back on the same page. But even when it's not struggling, keep a very close watch. I had a branch within my region that was not following our playbook, but they were just so nice to people, and they worked so hard that their service numbers were strong. But it wasn't sustainable, because all my data and experience told me that if they followed the protocols my managers and I had set down they would be even more successful with less work.

You address microcultures in the same way you address your larger culture. Identify them, acknowledge them, talk to the people involved in them, suggest constructive change, and implement that change around new goals and accountability standards.

SERVICE EXPRESS

How do you go about understanding and changing a culture in real time? Ron Alvesteffer is the president and CEO of data center company Service Express, which was chosen as one of 2020's Best Places to Work by Business Intelligence Group, and where 96 percent of employees said in a recent survey it's a great place to work, compared with a national average of 59 percent. His firm is an outstanding example of culture monitoring and assessment, and they use three key metrics to get the information they need.

They begin with core values, which equate to personal, professional, and financial goals. Like me, he's a fan of this famous Zig Ziglar quote: "You can get everything you want out of life, if you will just help enough other people get what they want." Twice a year employees and managers meet for "vision talks." Managers ask things like, "What do you love to do and see yourself doing at Service Express, and how does it fit into your personal life?" Ron told me he wants people to feel that because they work at Service Express they are able to achieve their goals.

The second metric is the four core objectives that the company runs on: double-digit revenue growth, which speaks for itself; keep growing margins, which is about being selective about the business they take on, not trying to be everything to everybody; employee engagement, which is about being the best company in the world to work for; and customer service, which is expressed in Net Promoter Score—the likelihood that a customer would recommend you to a friend or colleague. Ron says that when people make the decision to pursue these it's incredibly empowering for them.

Ron's third metric is the company's performance measurement system, SR5. It gives every employee a scorecard and scores them on their responsibilities, objectives, and indicators based on the company's quarterly priorities and objectives. The system is objective, creates alignment with strategies, and lets everyone know where they stand. It's part of the Service Express culture now.

Also, the company does online quarterly anonymous surveys, and every two years it conducts a companywide engagement survey. Ron's last survey showed that people thought the company was being more intentional about training and development, creating a pipeline of new leaders. That's a spectacular outcome.

Ron also does one more thing I really love. Every quarter he asks that his team read a book of their choice, and they're not all business books. He can't make people read them, but he can tell who is reading by their performance. In his view, the best employees are evolving as people, and that's what he wants, because if you're not evolving, the company will pass you by.

In the end, you need insight into your people's hearts and minds. You need to know what ingredients you're cooking with.

THE BRICKLAYER

If your surveys don't show any issues, you might not need this part of the process. But if you see trouble with six-point inspection data, you're showing warning lights. You need more data. That's when I'd suggest conducting additional employee surveys. Depending on the answers you get, you might need to pull the car over and make plans to do some serious cultural modification to your organization. How? By following the playbook in the previous chapters, of course! I've given you a chapter-by-chapter blueprint for doing it right. Just follow the road map, and you can't go wrong.

What are you ultimately looking for in your culture? I think the bricklayer parable makes that pretty clear. A man is walking by a construction site, but it's too early in the process to see what it's going to be. He comes across a bricklayer laying a course of bricks and asks, "Hey, buddy, what are you building?"

The bricklayer stops what he's doing, wipes away sweat, and says, "Man, I'm just laying a lot of bricks. I don't know." Then he goes back to his work. The man walks on, and a minute later he encounters another bricklayer working on a different side of the building. He's laid twice as many bricks as his counterpart. The man says, "Hey, what are you working on?"

This bricklayer looks at the man excitedly and says, "I'm building a cathedral!" then goes back to slapping mortar into a joint. Both men were doing the same job, but one had found meaning in the work, and that led him to engage with not only his hands but his heart.

A strong culture will give you employees like that second bricklayer. The culture grows from the inside, from your values and your employees, and eventually spreads to your customers, your community, the press, and even your shareholders. The power of clarity, trust, belief, authenticity, empowerment, discipline, consistency, awareness, and momentum are what make great culture possible.

There will be obstacles along the path, but when you stay true to the process something special happens. Nothing beats culture. *Nothing.* Build a strong one, and every other part of your business will be just as strong. This road map I have written about helped me and a number of the teams I was fortunate to be part of to create a truly special environment, a special place where individuals come together and do extraordinary things. But just like a road trip is nothing without the people in the car, this road map is all about you and your people and the talents and passion you all bring to your work. Take what I've given you, bring your gifts and skills and values to the table, and use this information to create something that changes your corner of the world for the better.

I wish you the best on your own road trip.

IN THE REARVIEW MIRROR

- Yes, you can check under the hood and quantitatively measure the health of your culture.
- The process has four parts: identify and understand your key cultural parts, watch for warning lights, perform diagnostics, and repair and renew the engine.
- Key cultural parts vary but usually include procedures, policies, advancement requirements, training and coaching, products, customers, technology, mission, and values.
- One important warning light is your culture's artifacts, behaviors, or cultural oddities unique to you that carry meaning.

- The key diagnostic tool is the six-point inspection system, which scores cultural health by looking at six critical components: engagement; customer satisfaction; values and ethics; diversity, equity, and inclusion; retention; and profit and revenue growth.
- You can repair your culture with some surprisingly simple initiatives.
- A strong culture is obvious to onlookers.
- You can adjust your cultural climate with meaningful ongoing initiatives.

AFTERWORD

've talked about culture consisting of certain beliefs, values, norms, and behaviors that create a unique and special experience or environment. Enterprise was one of those special places, and the way you know I'm sincere about that is my oldest son, Ryan, decided to launch his career at the very same place.

Ryan was going trick-or-treating to our administrative building at the age of about five. Then, as he grew, he would go to the summer picnic, and we would play basketball or volleyball with the team. He was maybe twelve or thirteen and saw this camaraderie and chemistry we all had together.

Another pivotal time for Ryan was the monthly elite dinner at our house, where we would recognize our top performers for the month. I wanted those to be a special experience for my employees. I wanted them to see my family and have a chance to interact with their fellow coworkers outside the normal work environment. Ryan was part of that. People would talk to Ryan and share stories with him. At that time Ryan already knew he would be attending the University of Rhode Island, and coincidentally, one of my all-star management assistants happened to know the captain of the Rhode Island football team and took it upon himself to reach out to Ryan and invite him to a game. My son got a great lesson in how to network, as well as one of my employees going out of his way to make my son feel like part of the team, which I really appreciated.

When he was in high school doing his capstone project—a final culminating research and writing project for graduating seniors— he wrote about a company. What company did he pick to write about? Enterprise, of course. He went through a training class and had a chance to listen and learn about the importance of providing excellent customer service and creating memorable moments throughout an interaction. He visited one of our busiest locations and observed how the employees prepared for a successful day and how training gets applied in real-world situations. I guess you could say he was already starting to follow a particular road map. When he got to Rhode Island, he decided to apply to be a customer assistant rep, and he was able to get hired. After that, he became an intern. Then, in 2020, Ryan was hired full time, in the very same region I used to lead.

It's now Ryan's turn to put his personal signature on his career and hopefully become the latest culture carrier. With some wise guidance and some sound choices, I believe he'll give both his own future, and my old employer, a jumpstart of their own.

ABOUT THE AUTHOR

E ric D. Stone's passion for business led him to a long and influential twenty-six-year career at the iconic rental car company Enterprise Holdings, one of the largest privately held companies in North America. Eric began his career as a Management Trainee in 1992 and quickly moved up the corporate ladder to become one of the most decorated Regional Vice Presidents in the company's history. His ability to connect and motivate employees from all different generations and demographics allowed his teams to sustain top-level results and a culture of pride. Eric attributes much of this success to his ability to create, build, and sustain a high-performance culture. It was this culture that enabled Eric to lead his teams through challenging times—including 9/11, the Great Recession, the COVID-19 pandemic, and the Great

Resignation—and his ability to adapt to the unexpected and to help others do the same became a hallmark of his management style. Eric retired from Enterprise in 2018 and founded Clear Path Ventures, which specializes in guiding young professionals and businesses as they navigate their path to success. From a community perspective, Eric has served on multiple boards in which he focuses on providing strategies and resources to close the opportunity gap for often-marginalized groups in the state of Connecticut.

ACKNOWLEDGMENTS

n order to be part of something special, there is always a long list of family, friends, employees, business partners, thought leaders, mentors, and advocates who have helped guide me along the journey. You've all taught me more than I could ever ask for.